MW00698348

STEVE CHAPMAN

The

BUCK
STOPS HERE

HARVEST HOUSE PUBLISHERS
EUGENE, OREGON

Every effort has been made to give proper credit for all stories, song lyrics, poems, and quotations. If for any reason proper credit has not been given, please notify the author or publisher, and proper notation will be given on future printing.

Cover design by Bryce Williamson

Cover photo © Alvarendra, PrettyVector, aleksandarvelasevic / GettyImages; stockcreations / Shutterstock

Interior design by KUHN Design Group

The Buck Stops Here
Copyright © 2021 by Steve Chapman
Published by Harvest House Publishers
Eugene, Oregon 97408
www.harvesthousepublishers.com

ISBN 978-0-7369-8290-0 (hardcover)
ISBN 978-0-7369-8291-7 (eBook)

Library of Congress Cataloging-in-Publication Data is on file at the Library of Congress, Washington, DC.

Printed in United States

21 22 23 24 25 26 27 28 / VP / 10 9 8 7 6 5 4 3 2 1

*My sincere thanks to those who have contributed
their wit and wisdom to these pages.*

Introduction

———❦———

The well-known statement "The buck stops here" has been around a long time. Popularized by President Harry Truman, it was a reference to the passing of a dealer marker in a game of poker.

If President Theodore Roosevelt had been the originator of the phrase, it might have quite a different meaning for one simple reason—he was an avid and skilled hunter who had stopped many bucks of the fur-covered kind in his day. Why do I think this is possible? Because I, too, am a huge fan of hunting, and the word *buck* doesn't conjure up the image of a marker or dollar in my head. I see whitetail deer and other antlered creatures.

Because of the likelihood that most other hunters react as I do when they hear "The buck stops here," it seemed like a good idea to enlist the attention-getting phrase as a title for this book. With my fellow fans of the fair chase in mind, I have filled the pages with…

- timeless quips and quotes about hunting that have been shared among those who enjoy the challenge of the pursuit. Some are humorous, some are serious, but all are included because they are memorable. Entries that are not my own are credited.

- hunting tips that can help make a trip to the woods and fields more successful.

- character-building insights that have been gleaned from experiences in the outdoors and can be applied to everyday life.

- short stories related to hunting that reveal why we love to do what we do and how engaging in our passion for the hunt serves to strengthen our relationships with family and friends.

And, because a lot of hunters opt to enjoy the outdoors by fishing during the off-season, there are some angling additions to the mix.

Two things to note about the format of this book:

1. The quips, quotes, tips, and stories do not appear in any particular order.

2. The majority of the entries are intentionally brief for a couple of reasons. I know the importance of lifting the eyes often to check the surroundings for approaching or passing critters. Short paragraphs

that require less time for the eyes to be down can make for more efficient hunting. And many of us prefer bumper-sticker-length readings anyway.

Each page of this book is purposely drenched with hunt-speak to bring a smile to a hunter's face, offer some wisdom, and provide the reader with an "aha" moment (or at the very least inspire another trip to the woods). Get ready and whisper, "The buck stops here!"

THE BUCK STOPS HERE

When I go hunting and come home empty-handed, I'm never disappointed. I just smile and say, "I had a great time, and I don't have to clean it."

❧ Deer Tip ❧

If there is a noticeable aroma generated by an agricultural industry (such as a pulp mill or dark-fired tobacco barns) in an area where deer are hunted, consider hanging up your camo outside to soak up the odor. Because the resident herd is very familiar with the smell and not as likely to be repelled by it, this "ambient odor tactic" could be useful in defeating the highly skilled olfactory system that a deer possesses.

SAY WHAT?

Hunters are often a misunderstood community of people, but it's no wonder, considering the strange meanings we've given to certain words and phrases.

- *Duck blind*: what we call a place where we can hide but still see the incoming birds.

- *Deer stand*: what we call a place where we sit— sometimes for hours.

- *Stalk*: a word in agriculture that refers to a motionless, standing plant. For hunters, this is a word we use for moving stealthily toward an animal we're pursuing.

- *Big game*: a major sporting event such as the Super Bowl, or an animal that's larger than small game.

- *Harvest*: the gathering of crops, or the hard reality of killing an animal.

- *Drive*: what is done with vehicles or what's inside computers. For hunters, it's what we do to push deer to a waiting buddy.

- *Rest*: For most of the world, this means sleeping. For hunters, it's a device on the riser of our bow that we put an arrow on before coming to full draw (draw, as in pull the string back, not using a pencil on paper). A rest can also be a backpack on a rock, which we use to steady our rifle for better accuracy on a long shot without scratching our forearm (on the gun, not our body) when the gun kicks after the trigger is pulled.

- *Guide*: a person who leads a group as they tour a famous sight. For hunters, this is someone who helps us use our sights.

- *Cover scent*: a pleasant, aromatic spray in an aerosol can, found on the lid of a commode tank and used for masking residual, foul human odors. For hunters, a cover scent can be a very unpleasant odor in a little bottle used for masking the lingering pleasant smell of a human.

- *Opening day*: when the masses can go inside a brand-new store and shop for items such as groceries. For hunters, it's when we can go into the ageless outdoors and "shop" for food.

- *Biggest fan*: a celebrity's most ardent admirer. For turkey hunters, it's the tail plumage on the heaviest gobbler we ever "harvested."

RECORDS BOOKS

D eer hunters who hunt doe only because they favor the meat more than the potentially gamy buck are somewhat rare and should always be respected for their preference. Sadly, they have no representation in records books such as *Boone and Crockett* (for firearm kills) or *Pope and Young* (for archery kills) due to their focus on antler size, total points, and trophy-level scoring. To solve this unfortunate oversight, perhaps there should be the establishment of companion records books to the two mentioned above. They could be called *Boom and Cook It* and *Poke and Yummy*.

I hope no one labours under the delusion that hunting is a mere barbarous, bloodthirsty sport. Every good hunter will agree with me that it is not the killing of the animal that gives pleasure. The charm lies in overcoming difficulties—in matching your natural intelligence and acquired knowledge and skill against the instinct, cunning, intellect, and reason of the animal you are endeavoring to outwit.

THE EARL OF DUNRAVEN

He who waits for a roast duck to fly into his mouth must wait a very, very long time.

CHINESE PROVERB

Hunter's Hint

Two or three small candles are well worth packing for a backcountry hunting trip. They make for quick and easy emergency lights, and they can help start a fire with damp or stubborn kindling. Further, softened candle wax can be used to temporarily treat a broken tooth or as an emergency replacement for a lost filling.

ANNIE ON THE MARK

Annie Oakley's marksmanship, honed by years of hunting, made her a celebrity by the time she was a teenager. At 15 she defeated professional marksman Frank Butler in a shooting exhibition. A year later they married, and Butler eventually became his five-foot wife's assistant in the traveling Buffalo Bill's Wild West show. As part of her act, Annie shot a dime out of the air and a cigarette from her husband's mouth. She could also hit a playing card thrown into the air from a distance of 90 feet.

Deer Tip

If you haven't seen a deer during archery season after sitting in your tree stand all morning, try this: Attach your pull-up string to your bow and lower the bow to the ground. Once you have it a little over halfway down, a nice shooter buck should appear. I've seen it work more than once.

"PLEASE EXCUSE DAVY
FROM SCHOOL"

S chools across the country allow a "hunting vacation" for students. However, famed frontiersman Davy Crockett holds the unofficial record for the longest "hunting vacation." At the age of 13, he ran away from home and lived off the land for more than two years. The reason? He wanted to avoid being punished for playing hooky.

*However much you knock at nature's door, she will
never answer you in comprehensible words.*

IVAN TURGENEV, *ON THE EVE*

Hunter's Bible

*"I am an old man now," Isaac said, "and I don't know when
I may die. Take your bow and a quiver full of arrows, and
go out into the open country to hunt some wild game for me.
Prepare my favorite dish, and bring it here for me to eat."*

GENESIS 27:2-4 NLT

*Depend on the rabbit's foot if you will, but
remember it didn't work for the rabbit.*

R.E. Shay

IT'S ALL IN THE LEGS—
BUT NOT ALWAYS

According to research, leg strength is an important factor in archery success. While this may be true for tournament shooting, there are at least three good reasons for a hunter to learn to shoot a bow while seated. Not standing up to take a shot can help outwit the keen eyes of an animal by minimizing movement and profile; it can help avoid the mistake of alerting their well-trained ears by eliminating noises such as a creaking stand or, for older hunters, popping knees; and it can save valuable seconds of preparation when the animal appears unexpectedly.

SADDLED WITH A LOUSY JOB?

American frontiersman Kit Carson embarked on his career as a hunter and guide after he was sent to work for a Missouri saddlemaker. Carson hated the job so much that he ran away, around age 17, with a group of traders headed for what is now Santa Fe, New Mexico.

I went to the woods because I wished to live deliberately, to front only the essential facts of life, and see if I could not learn what it had to teach, and not, when I came to die, discover that I had not lived.

HENRY DAVID THOREAU

God gives us our relatives, but thank heaven we can choose our hunting and fishing buddies.

TIM HANSON

Hunter's Hint

Whoever originally said, "Clothes make the man," I totally agree with him—but only as a hunter. I recommend taking your choice of attire seriously when it comes to getting dressed for hunting success. For example, the fabric should feature a camo pattern appropriate for the area and time of year. For blending purposes when it's winter and the trees are leafless, allowing more sunshine in the woods, opt for a lighter hue of camo. In the early fall and late spring when the foliage is fuller, creating more shadows, transition to a darker shade of camo. And, because a productive hunt sometimes requires a longer stay outdoors, it's imperative to choose clothing that will help you endure any challenging weather conditions.

NOT THE SHARPEST
ARROW IN THE QUIVER

I lost the first two turkeys I shot with archery equipment because the razor-sharp broadheads I used (not the expandable type) slipped through them and, though wounded, they flew off—never to be seen again. That's when I decided to switch to tipping my arrow with a Judo point, which is designed for target practice.

Instead of a pass through, a Judo point impact yields penetration along with a shock-and-roll result. My change to this effective method may have been for the same reason that some ancient Native Americans chose to use unsharpened arrows to hunt birds found in trees. Their arrows stunned the perched target so that they tumbled to the ground, where they could be dispatched easily. While I shoot gobblers only at ground level, I can report that the wide-faced, clawed Judo point has not yielded another lost bird.

A TAXING TRUTH

By paying surtaxes on guns, ammo, and other gear, hunters send hundreds of millions of dollars to state conservation programs each year.

*One loyal hunting dog is worth
a truckload of in-laws.*

TAYLOR MORGAN

OUTDOOR-TOUGH

President Theodore Roosevelt's outdoorsman lifestyle made him one tough customer. How tough? While campaigning for a return to the White House in 1912, he was shot by a saloonkeeper. With the bullet still lodged in his chest, Roosevelt delivered his campaign speech as scheduled.

All hunters should be nature lovers.

THEODORE ROOSEVELT

HOLDING HISTORY

In my nearly six decades of hunting, there have been only a few occasions when I have had the opportunity to hold history in my hand. By that I mean finding an arrowhead at my feet, picking it up, and doing what I always do when I make such a rare find. Whether I'm holding a whole or broken portion of an arrowhead, I like to stand for a few minutes, look at it, and take in the realization that in my hand is a connection to someone who lived on the ground where I'm standing hundreds of years ago.

I imagine who last held the small, hand-shaped flint—their name, their life span, and the kind of existence they had. I wonder if the arrowhead was used for hunting or for war. The moment also makes me look ahead to a time many years from now when one of my metal broadheads might be found by a future hunter. Will he take the time to imagine who last touched it? Perhaps his weaponry will be so advanced that he'll look at my broadhead and say the same thing I do when I hold a flint arrowhead in my hand: "How in the world did anyone hunt with these things?"

THE VEGGIE TRAP

Some anti-hunting crusaders aren't aware of it, but every vegetable farm in the world has to kill or trap animals, such as rabbits and deer, in order to protect its crops.

A business consultant is like a guy who comes out from the trees to shoot the carcass after the hunt is over.

LAWRENCE BRINK

The only reason I played golf was so that I could afford to go hunting and fishing.

SAM SNEAD, LEGENDARY PRO GOLFER

OFF TO THE WOODS

As an avid hunter and wannabe-better golfer, I've discovered a fact that, for me, is undeniable. Golf and hunting are alike in that both involve going to the woods and looking for something.

THE BEAR FACTS

Hunting increases a bear cub's chances of survival. A study by the University of Alberta found that cubs have a 25 percent better chance of survival in an area where black bear hunting is allowed than in a region where it is prohibited. The reason: Large male bears, the ones hunters seek, prey on cubs.

SAVING LIVES, SAVING MONEY

It's my contention that controlling the deer population by allowing deer hunting can save your life and save you money. How? Deer hunting means fewer deer that are killed by cars. Deer-automobile collisions annually kill about 200 people, which is more than the number of people who are killed each year by sharks, cougars, bears, and alligators combined. Moreover, the yearly 1.5 million deer-vehicle collisions in the United States costs the insurance industry more than $1 billion.

Nature, to be commanded, must be obeyed.

FRANCIS BACON

"YOU'RE WELCOME, MR. CATTLE"

I was invited to keynote at a two-night wild game dinner event in Pennsylvania where a room full of hungry attendees were served venison each evening. I learned that it took 12 deer to meet the total demand of 700 pounds of meat. That being the case, there were two 800-1,000 pound steers that owed a big debt of gratitude to those dozen deer.

FEEDING THE HUNGRY

During a recent seven-year period, Farmers and Hunters Feeding the Hungry processed 1,600 tons of venison and other big game for soup kitchens and food pantries nationwide. The amount of meat processed equals almost 13 million servings of food.

PLAYING IT SAFE

Statistically speaking, hunting is safer for a kid than other sports. According to American Sports Data, Inc., 13.8 percent of sports injuries annually are from basketball, 8.2 percent from running, and 1.4 percent from golf. Hunting represents 1 percent of the total, an even lower percentage than ping-pong.

WOMEN ON THE HUNT

According to the National Sporting Goods Association, 72 percent more women are hunting today than just five years ago. (According to a 2016 survey, more than three million women hunt with firearms annually.)

IF AT FIRST YOU DON'T SUCCEED...HUNT!

After several failed business ventures, William Frederick Cody became a buffalo hunter, supplying meat for railroad workmen. His skill as a hunter—legend has it that he killed more than 4,000 buffalo in 8 months—earned him the nickname "Buffalo Bill."

DE-DUCK-TIVE REASONING

Whoever said, "A bad day of duck hunting is better than a good day at the office," has obviously had both and should be especially grateful for the latter—otherwise, the financial resources needed to enjoy a day of duck hunting might not be available.

A BEAR HUNTER NAMED
BOONE (OR BOON)

Daniel Boone would carve an inscription into a tree after killing a bear. The inscriptions reveal that he was a much better hunter than a scholar. He would render *bear* as *bar* and sometimes misspell his own surname.

Hunter's Hint

Until you are accurate enough with your handgun to place all your bullets into an 8-inch paper plate (or similar target) at 50 to 75 yards, you are not ready to hunt big game with that handgun.

 Outdoor Poetry

Alone far in the wilds and mountains I hunt,
Wandering amazed at my own lightness and glee,
In the late afternoon choosing a safe spot to pass the night,
Kindling a fire and broiling the fresh-kill'd game,
Falling asleep on the gather'd leaves with
my dog and gun by my side.

WALT WHITMAN, "SONG OF MYSELF"

Hunter's Bible

The meat you eat may be butchered anywhere, just
as you do now with gazelle and deer. Eat as much
of this meat as you wish and as often as you are able
to obtain it, because the Lord has prospered you.

DEUTERONOMY 12:15 TLB

A FEW FERAL FACTS

- A feral hog is one that has returned to an untamed state from a domesticated state.

- Feral hogs stink terribly, but their ability to smell keenly is not affected.

- Their sensitive hearing is not hampered by their noisy grunting and snorting as they dig the ground with their hooves and root in the mud with their snouts in search of grubs and other food sources. The slightest strange sound can stop them mid-chomp and send them scampering.

- Though ugly, wild hogs are very intelligent. (I can relate to that!)

- The females are mature enough to breed by the time they reach ten months of age—sometimes sooner. They can birth six or more piglets once or twice a year, making the feral hog the most prolific large mammal on the planet.

- Swine are not native to our nation. They were introduced to North America by Spanish explorers and became feral when they either were abandoned by their owners or simply wandered away.

- The feral hog is considered a destructive pest, and open seasons exist for hunters who want to pursue them. Often there is no limit to the number that can be killed.

*The two best times to fish is when it's
raining and when it ain't.*

PATRICK McMANUS

LITTLE SURE SHOT

Annie Oakley learned to shoot at age eight, and, as a child, helped support her family by killing game for a local store. In her later years, she performed shooting exhibitions for the US military during World War I.

NICE COAT, DEER

The hollow hairs that constitute a whitetail deer's winter coat are as good as or better at insulating than the most sophisticated high-tech fiber that humankind has developed. These deer live as far north as the fifty-ninth parallel, where winter temperatures routinely plunge to –60°F.[1]

NATURE'S PICTURE OF UNITY

Our beautiful forests are made up of many types of trees. While they vary greatly in size, shape, and appearance, each one draws strength and nourishment from the same soil. And, without jealousy or conflict, they stand side by side—each fulfilling its individual purpose of contributing bounty and shelter to all the forest residents. Wouldn't it be great if all churches were like trees?

FAVORITE OUTDOOR SMELL

On the morning of my very first hunt I was introduced to my all-time favorite outdoor aroma. In a pre-dawn moment, the gentleman who took me on a squirrel hunt used his boot to scrape away the leaf-laden ground cover that was under a huge oak. As I sat down, the distinct, pungent aroma of the moist, raw earth filled the air—and my heart as well.

These many years later I often say, "If I'm ever in a coma, grab either a handful of well-aged, leaf-covered dirt or some Hunters Specialties 'fresh earth cover' scent wafers, come to the hospital, and wave either of them under my nose. Then watch me sit up and smile!"

SACRIFICE

The first recorded killing of an animal is in the Old Testament. After Adam and Eve sinned in the Garden of Eden, "the eyes of both were opened, and they knew that they were naked. And they sewed fig leaves together and made themselves loincloths" (Genesis 3:7 ESV).

Their self-made covering was temporary at best. When God entered the garden, He provided a covering for them that would be long-lasting. We learn that "the LORD God made for Adam and for his wife garments of skins and clothed them" (Genesis 3:21 ESV).

Some scholars of the Bible think that likely the animal from which the skins were made was a lamb. Assuming so, two striking observations can be made. God showed Adam and Eve that the shedding of blood was required to cover their shame—and pointed to the future, when it would be said of His Son, "Behold, the Lamb of God, who takes away the sin of the world!" (John 1:29 ESV).

JOYS DOUBLED,
SORROWS HALVED

The well-known saying, "With friends joys are doubled and sorrows are halved," is especially true for hunters. When something goes awfully bad, such as missing a shot at a trophy of a lifetime, nothing is as consoling as the kind and understanding words of a friend. But how doubly sweet are the high fives—and even tens—that are shared by friends after a successful hunt.

CONCRETE SCARS

If you've ever felt the hurt that comes when a great hunting property is taken by the construction of a paved highway, then we have something in common. When the big machines finish cutting through the fields and forests where cherished hunting memories were made, what remains is a deep wound permanently marked by a concrete scar.

THE WONDER OF THE WEB

Have you ever sat in the woods on an early autumn deer hunt or on a warm spring day during gobbler season and watched a spider quietly and patiently weave a web? If so, you've seen a true artist at work using a skill that was instilled by its Maker. As you watched, did it occur to you that your Creator has also given *you* an amazing skill? What is it? Have you discovered it yet? I hope so, because someone could be as inspired by watching you use your skill as you were by seeing the spider use its artistic talent.

It takes one to hunt one.

ANNIE CHAPMAN, ON TURKEY HUNTING

IN A LEGEND'S PRESENCE

D on't let being unable to do something better keep you from doing your best." This statement by Vance Havner is one I have used to encourage myself when I'm faced with doing something in the presence of someone who is obviously much more skilled at the task than I am. This quote served me well, for example, when I felt intimidated while sitting next to legendary hunter and Alaska brown-bear guide Dale Adams, who monitored my every move as a monstrous brownie approached. The result of giving the challenge my best shot even though Adams was watching is now hanging on the wall in my man cave in the form of a huge bear rug.

By the way, Adams not only calmly coached me through the hunt, but he also made me feel quite at ease around him—the mark of a gracious guide.

I NEED MEDS

T he itch to go hunting cannot be scratched at home—and using hunting shows to relieve the itch just makes it worse. The only cure is a cocktail of meds made up of an open season, leaving the house, and heading to the woods.

YOU'VE BEEN HAD

Me, with an opening question as keynote speaker at a church-sponsored wild game dinner: "How many of you like *wild turkey?*"

Audience response: Many hands instantly go up.

Me, before the hands go down: "Uh…I mean—the bird!"

Audience response: Nervous laughter, many hands are quickly lowered.

Me: "We're in church. You shouldn't have gotten that joke."

Audience response: Thankfully, more laughter.

Hunter's Bible

"Now I will send for many fishermen," declares the
LORD, "and they will catch them. After that I will send for
many hunters, and they will hunt them down on every
mountain and hill and from the crevices of the rocks."

JEREMIAH 16:16 NIV

❧ Deer Tip ❧

To help a young hunter understand how skilled a white-tail's nose is, I would say that a deer can smell odors the way humans can see colors. They have no problem differentiating between natural and unnatural aromas. For that reason, my advice is to use human scent suppression, such as bathing in scentless soap and wearing camo that has been aromatically neutralized as much as possible.

But these measures, as important and necessary as they may be, are not enough—and I'd credit the late and legendary deer-hunting expert Charles J. Alsheimer for the extra wisdom. Years ago he told me, "Steve, nothing works better than hunting into the wind when it comes to outsmarting a deer's nose. No matter how well prepared you are with your costly, scent-free camo and pH-factor eliminating spray, you still have to breathe. And if you are, you're busted, because a deer can smell even the toothpaste you used before you left your house to go to the woods."

Let Charlie's words echo in your head each time you arrive at the place where you'll hunt. Before you take a step away from your vehicle, check the wind direction and let it tell you where to take a stand.

IF HUNTING WERE BANNED

If hunting were banned as we know it today, based on the damage I've seen animals make on planted fields, it wouldn't surprise me if in five to ten years we'd have no crops to harvest.

WIRED TO DO IT

It seems that God wires people to enjoy certain activities. For me it's hunting, fishing, and simply being outdoors. I've found that He uses my interests as a way to teach me and guide me to becoming a better man. It happens especially when I see truths in His written Word illustrated in creation or when I see realities in nature that are confirmed in His Word.

RIGHTLY DIVIDE THE RABBITS

If you field dress rabbits for the family down the road, and you use plastic grocery bags to separate the edible meat from the innards, make sure you take the right bag to the neighbors. The wrong bag can send them an unwanted message. I speak from experience.

⊰✦ Outdoor Poetry ✦⊱

Here in these woods of Tennessee
In the early part of May
Though spring I saw a youthful leaf
Fall on this warm day

It seems so sad while in its green
For a leaf so new to die
And miss its place among the scenes
Of the autumn colors bright

The same is true for every child
Who leaves when they are young
We'll miss the colors of their smile
When their October comes[2]

NO HUNTING

A "No Hunting" sign is not a restriction. It's an opportunity to exercise the freedom to engage in self-discipline.

ER REALITY CHECK

On the first day of deer season a hunter fell out of his tree stand and broke both legs. Complaining to the emergency room doctor, the hunter asked, "Why couldn't this have happened on my last day of hunting?" His doctor said, "It did!"[3]

What's the difference between a hunter and a fisherman?
A hunter lies in wait while a fisherman waits and lies.

AUTHOR UNKNOWN

⊰ Outdoor Poetry ⊱

When the green of the cornstalk begins to turn brown
When the time for the goldenrod bloom comes around
That's when I look to the hills for I know
Soon I'll walk there again with my arrow and bow
When the fruit of the white oak is ready to fall
When the hummingbird feels that old Mexico call
And when tears touch the cheeks of my sweetheart, she knows
Soon it's farewell to her man with the arrow and bow
The heart of the hunter, who can explain
How the first winds of autumn seem to whisper my name?
And they send me to dreaming 'bout the morning I'll go
Back up to the hills with my arrow and bow[4]

*Everything you take into the field—your rifle or
bow, your backpack, your camo gear, your food,
yourself—everything is piled on top of your boots. The
bottom line is: Don't go cheap on your boots.*

JAY HOUSTON

EQUAL-CASH METHOD

There's a way that a smart husband can help his wife not resent what he spends on hunting gear—and even help her appreciate his passion for hunting. It's called the "equal-cash method." If, for example, the husband buys a new mechanical release and set of sight pins for his bow, he could then go to the bank and withdraw the same amount he spent in cash and give it to his wife. This self-imposed policy will not only send her a message that he's thinking of her feelings about outlay, but it'll also help curb his spending.

Important disclaimer: This equal-cash method is not recommended when it comes to the purchase of large items—such as a 19-foot, fiberglass, fully decked-out bass boat, complete with a two-axle trailer and a new four-wheel-drive pickup to pull it all. A purchase like this should be a mutual decision. This, too, can help a marriage.

MEME TRUTH

A message posted on a well-circulated meme with a photo of a huge, vicious-looking grizzly bear: "What doesn't kill you makes you stronger. Except for bears. Bears will kill you." True—and they'll eat you too!

Deer Tip

If you're sitting on the ground, at eye level with a deer's vision, and you have to scratch your nose, adjust your facemask, raise your binoculars to your eyes, or move your hands for any other reason, don't raise them quickly in a straight line. Instead, mimic the gentle swaying of leaves in the breeze and bring your hands to your face slowly, with slight side-to-side movements.

TO BE A MAN

You don't have to be a man to hunt, and you don't have to hunt to be a man.

THEY'RE STILL HERE

I was utterly disappointed when I walked onto a farm in July that I've hunted for several years and discovered what the loggers had done. Gone were the big trees that had provided cooling shade in the warm, early weeks of archery season and a plentiful, annual crop of acorns—as well as straight trunks where I could place my deer stands. All that was left were the tops of the trees lying on the ground in a tangled mess that only a snake could slither through.

As I took in the sight of such devastation, I thought about the season ahead and felt mournful that I would have to eliminate the property from my short list of locations where I could hunt.

But then I revisited the farm about a month later, after the loggers were gone, and walked the roads they had cut through the area. I was totally surprised by what I found. The soft, bare dirt of the logging roads had several sets of deer tracks on them, and some were obviously made by sizable bucks. And when I got off the roads to explore the ground clutter created by the dozens of massive treetops, I found deer trails. It was amazing to see how they had adapted to the chainsaw carnage and woven their way through the chaos.

In total amazement at what I saw, I whispered, "They're still here! They have a thousand places to hide. This is not devastation. This place is a deer haven!" I was a happy hunter—and I'll never think badly of a logger again.

⚞ Hunter's Hint ⚟

When still-hunting, always watch where you place each foot to make sure you don't step on a fallen stick that would crack loudly when it breaks and consequently give away your presence. If you take a step where it appeared there were only leaves, but you feel a stick underneath your foot, deliberately avoid putting all your weight on it if possible.

A SONG IN THE QUAIL

It is generally accepted that the fowl God sent for food into the wilderness camp of the Israelites (see Exodus 16 and Numbers 11) was a bird akin to a quail. In that small bird is an illustration of a song. The wings can be compared to the music, and the breast meat is a picture of the lyrics. A song needs strong wings to get the meat of the message to a hungry heart.

SHOOTING STRAIGHT
WITH A CROOKED BOW

It's not how straight the stave is that makes an accurate shooting bow—it's how much the bowyer knows about working with misshapen wood. The same is true with God and people. Most of us are warped by life in one way or another, but God knows how to work with our imperfections. He can shoot straight with crooked bows.

HUNTING SUCCESS

Sometimes, success as a hunter is determined not by how close I can get to the animal I'm pursuing, but how far away from it I can get if I'm needed at home.

BEING HUNTED

I've tried to imagine what a deer feels when it suddenly realizes that someone or something is pursuing it. The way its tail flares up and its body crouches in readiness to spring into an escape makes me wonder if it is not only responding to an instinct to survive, but if there is a humanlike fear that grips its mind. Whatever the case may be, deer obviously react to being hunted.[5]

Hunter's Bible

Now Cush became the father of Nimrod; he became a mighty one on the earth. He was a mighty hunter before the LORD; therefore it is said, "Like Nimrod a mighty hunter before the LORD."

GENESIS 10:8-9

OVERHEARD IN THE FOYER

After one of our concerts that included a couple of hunting illustrations, a song about baseball, and plenty of talk about God, my wife, Annie, overheard a man in the foyer say to his friend, "I didn't wanna come tonight, but I heard about hunting, God, and baseball... It just don't get any better than that!"

VACATION MINUTES

Five minutes of sleep in a deer stand is like a week of vacation.

Hunter's Bible

There are three things that are too amazing for me,
four that I do not understand:
the way of an eagle in the sky,
the way of a snake on a rock,
the way of a ship on the high seas,
and the way of a man with a young woman.

PROVERBS 30:18-19 NIV

A VALID ARGUMENT?

With food supplies being plentiful and quite accessible, it seems that we've come to a time in American history when, for most of us, hunting is no longer necessary for survival. Instead, hunting is a chosen pastime. This modern reality is often included in the arsenal of word-weapons used by those who contend that hunting is a cruel act of violence against other living things and should be outlawed. The truth is that their argument has validity—until they deliberately bite into a fried chicken leg or a cut of prime rib. End of debate.

LEARNING THE DIFFERENCE

Being able to tell the difference between the scamper of a squirrel and a deer's hooves carefully pressing into dry leaves is a skill learned only through time and experience. The first time I was able to "just know" if a yet-to-be-seen critter was one or the other was very satisfying.

CALLED IN

When I use my grunt call to entice a buck within shooting range of my bow, my intent is to kill him. When God called me to Himself using His voice of mercy, His intent was to give me life eternal. I'm grateful to say that in both cases, the call worked.[6]

WAY OUT OF TOWN

For most of us, hunting takes place close to the boundary of a city. We're never really far enough away from civilization to rightly claim we've gone into the wilderness. But when we do get the opportunity to go dangerously deep into nature, and we seize it, a part of our heart is left out there—and we'll always want to go back to visit it.

When you share meat from a deer, or a duck, or
a fish you have killed, you are participating
in an essential human sacrament.

SHANE MAHONEY, *OUTDOOR LIFE*

FAIR CHASE

The word *sport* has varied implications, including play, use of developed skills, rules, regulations, competitions, and awards. Based on these descriptions, hunting could be referred to as a sport since it…

- requires skill in handling a firearm or bow.

- involves state and federal rules regarding when, where, and how to hunt as well as how many of a species can be taken.

- includes a battle of wits that takes place between the hunter and the hunted.

Though these similarities exist, only the human gets to categorize hunting as a sport. To the animal, it's a serious matter of life and death. For that reason, I prefer not to refer to hunting as a sport, since in a sport both sides should know they're in the game.

Instead, when the rules and regulations are followed closely (for example, restricting weapon size and type, hunting only during the daytime and in season, obeying bag limits, etc.), the activity of hunting can be more accurately called the "fair chase."

LIVE TO HUNT OR HUNT TO LIVE

Davy Crockett, the legendary outdoorsman hailing from an area of America that eventually would be called the state of Tennessee, claimed to have killed 105 black bears during the winter of 1825–1826. By today's standards, laws, and bag limits, that number may sound excessive and even unethical. But Crockett didn't just live to hunt—he would hunt to live!

Hunter's Bible

The slothful man roasteth not that which he took in hunting: but the substance of a diligent man is precious.

PROVERBS 12:27 KJV

Translation: A slothful man won't have meat to eat because he's either too lazy to go hunting or too lazy to clean and cook the animal after he kills it (or both). On the other hand, those who are industrious and hard working will enjoy the fruit—the backstraps and tenderloins—of their diligent labor.

SNARES AND TRAPS
IN BIBLICAL DAYS

There are many uses of the words *snare* and *trap* in both the Old and New Testaments. For example, "Surely he shall deliver thee from the snare of the fowler" (Psalm 91:3 KJV), and "Those who want to be rich fall into temptation and are trapped by many senseless and harmful desires" (1 Timothy 6:9 NRSV). The logical conclusion is that snares and traps were common in Bible days and served as useful metaphors in guiding hearers and readers to an understanding of greater truths—otherwise, reference to them would have had no impact.

GOD AS HUNTER

Job referred to God as a hunter when he said, "You would hunt me like a lion" (10:16), and "God…has closed His net around me" (19:6).

FIRST BLOOD

The first discovery of blood on the ground after taking a shot at a deer is the moment when a convergence of several very intense emotions takes place. These emotions include the excitement of the encounter, the relief of knowing the bullet or arrow connected with the animal's flesh, the high hope that the carcass will be found, and the sobering thought that the animal has suffered at the hunter's hand. Then when—or if—the animal is found, the excitement will be over, and the work will begin.

PILOTS AND DEER HUNTERS

Airline pilots and tree-stand deer hunters have one thing in common: They're both above ground when they do what they do. Other than that, their experiences are opposite since flying, according to one pilot I spoke to, is hours and hours of boredom interrupted by moments of stark fear. Not so for deer hunting, which is hours and hours of sweet anticipation interrupted by moments of incredible excitement.

DROPPING NUMBERS

The number of hunters who head to the woods each year seems to be dropping. There are likely two significant causes for this reduction.

- *The breakdown of the family.* Hunting is an interest that is very often passed from one family member to another, such as a father to his child, grandparent to a grandkid, or an uncle to a nephew or niece. If a family breaks apart due to separation, divorce, or other causes, they likely won't pass on the heritage of hunting.

- *The loss of land.* With large sections of property being bought for industrial and residential use, along with huge tracts of land being developed by private "pay to hunt" companies, it is becoming more of a challenge to find places to hunt independently. Consequently, many hunters simply give up and move on to other more attainable interests.

Hunter's Bible

Indeed, it is useless to spread the baited net
In the sight of any bird;
But they lie in wait for their own blood;
They ambush their own lives.
So are the ways of everyone who gains by violence;
It takes away the life of its possessors.

Proverbs 1:17-19

FLASHLIGHT WISDOM

A working flashlight is not only good for making safe predawn treks into the woods and post-sunset exits, but it's also an excellent illustration of an undeniable truth. In the same way that a flashlight is worthless without a battery, my shell of a life is meaningless without the power of God's love inside, making me shine with the light of compassion for others.

TURKEY EYES

I t is said that a turkey's eyes intensely magnify the images they see. If so, maybe their gobbling is not a mating call after all but a reaction to everything seeming so close and huge to them. Perhaps they should have a message on the inside of their eyelids that says, "Warning! Things are farther away than they appear."

Deer Tip

D eer can communicate with each other in more ways than one, and a wise hunter can gain an advantage by learning their unique languages.

Vocal

- A doe will *grunt* to let a fawn know its mother is near. The volume starts low but can rise if the fawn does not respond.

- A very young fawn will *mew* sort of like a kitten and *whine* while nursing, as well as *bleat* when lost or *bawl* when significantly stressed.

- Both a doe and a buck will *snort* when only moderately alarmed and sometimes *repeatedly snort* when trouble is sensed but not yet identified. They'll *bawl* loudly when intensely scared or under attack.

- A buck's best-known vocalization is *grunting*. Used mostly during the breeding periods, a dominant buck will issue a low-pitched grunt, while a younger buck's pitch is higher. When bucks become hostile to one another as they compete for a doe in heat, their grunting may be coupled with a snort (*grunt-snort*). When they get highly aggressive toward one another, they'll add a *wheeze* to the mix (*grunt-snort-wheeze*). The *tending grunt*, the sound a buck makes when trailing the scent of a "hot" doe, is especially familiar and welcomed to a seasoned deer hunter.

Visual

Both sexes of deer often use a *foot stomp* in reaction to a sudden feeling of alarm. It's a definite sign to surrounding deer, as well as to the source of alarm, that the animal senses danger—but not quite enough yet to flee. Additional visual methods that both female and male deer use include…

- *lowered tail wagging* (relaxed)

- *stationary raised tail along with a standing stare* (very concerned)

- *lowered tail after being raised* (convinced of a false alarm)

- *raised tail flagging* (extremely alarmed—usually seen

when a deer is escaping perceived danger, as if waving goodbye)

- *ear drop* (dramatically raised aggression level, often accompanied by *widened eyes*, *flared nostrils*, *raised fur*, and *flattened tail*)

Olfactory

- Does will use their *fawn's natural odor* to keep track of them. Also, a doe in estrus (ready for breeding) will emit a *hormone-produced smell* that attracts a buck. Does let it be known that they are in estrus by urinating in a ground scrape made by a potential mating buck.

- Bucks *urinate on their tarsal gland* located on the inside of their back legs. The pungent smell created by this unusual trait is strong and can be detectable by a hunter with a trained, experienced nose. Bucks also rub their *forehead gland* on trees near head level, leaving an odorous indicator of their breeding desire.

There are other aspects of deer languages that could be added, but understanding just the few mentioned here will keep you busy until the time your hunting days are over.

SUMMARY SEASON

D ads who have small children and who are also avid hunters can make great use of the time between the last day of turkey season in the spring and the opening day of deer season in the fall. These song lyrics will tell you how.

Just Add Water

*If you wanna make a sweet memory
with your kid, here's the recipe*

*Peanut butter and a jar of jam,
loaf of bread and pop in a can*

*Bamboo poles and hooks on the line,
a can of worms and some of your time*

*And don't forget that little round bobber,
then all you do is just add water*

Just add water, don't have to be deep

Take 'em to the banks of a big lake or a little creek

Sweet memories with your sons and your daughters

That's what you'll get when you just add water

*You can take your phone but leave it off,
turn on your heart and let it talk*

*'Cause words come easy when you're fishing,
and when they talk make sure you listen*

And if the weather turns hot and the fish go hide,
don't pack it up and run back inside

Just tell the kids to do like their father;
roll up your pants and just add water[7]

THE SLEEP CHALLENGER

The last time I went to sleep easily the night before a hunt was in October of 1963. It was the night before my very first outing. I had no idea that the excitement of such an experience awaiting me when I woke up would, from then on, challenge my ability to fall asleep quickly.

TREE ALTAR

A tree stand is a great place to pray because you're closer to God.

⇥ Outdoor Poetry ⇤

He was 12 years old, sitting with his grandpa
Underneath that big oak tree way up in the hollow
Watching for whitetail in that November sun
Holding on tight to that Winchester gun

They started talking and kept it to a whisper
About beagles and baseball and putting up with sisters
Then like a wise old hunter his grandpa said,
"As long you live, boy, don't you forget…

"God's gonna keep you in his sights
He'll be lookin' out for you; you're precious in His eyes
Wherever you go on the trail of this life, you'll be all right
'Cause God's gonna keep you in His sights"

Year after year they were in those hills together
Makin' those memories, the kind that last forever
Then came the season when the world went to war
The boy was just 19 when he landed on that shore

And in that moment, way down in his soul
He could hear his grandpa's voice coming from that hollow
Saying…
"God's gonna keep you in His sights
He'll be lookin' out for you; you're precious in His eyes
Wherever you go on the trail of this life, you'll be all right
'Cause God's gonna keep you in His sights"[8]

A MAJOR FAST

Fasting is not an easy discipline to follow, but the benefits—especially when combined with praying—are undeniable. I knew a man who felt compelled to add fasting to his prayers for his kids, and instead of giving up food, he decided to sacrifice an entire hunting season. That would be a gargantuan challenge for me. The children of that brave and dedicated dad surely must have become missionaries in a faraway land—maybe even on Mars!

Deer Tip

Whether you're hunting deer with a bow or gun, avoid wearing your camo into your kitchen at home or at deer camp while cooking breakfast (especially if bacon or sausage is on the menu). Also, don't wear your camo when going into a convenience store or a fast-food eatery on the way to your hunting ground. The odors that fill those places (and others like them) will cling to the material and can easily be detected by the sensitive nose of the deer. Instead, store the camo in a sealed plastic bag and then dress at the hunt site just before heading to your stand.

Hunter's Bible

These are the animals you may eat: the ox, the sheep, the goat, the deer, the gazelle, the roe deer, the wild goat, the ibex, the antelope and the mountain sheep.

DEUTERONOMY 14:4-5 NIV

Note that on this Old Testament list of acceptable animals that could be consumed, some could be obtained only by being hunted, thus giving implied biblical approval of hunting as a way to provide food.

A DUCK BLIND DESCRIBED

Here's a description of a duck blind filled with friends, food, and a lot of feathers flying overhead:

Bite, sip, bite, talk, quack, quack, "Take 'em!" boom, boom, splash, "Go get 'em, dog," bite, quack, quack, boom, boom, chew, sip, boom, boom, splash, splash, "Go get 'em," boom, joke, laughter, boom, boom, bite, chew, trash talk, laughing, boom, boom.

❧ Hunter's Hint ❧

A tick is essentially an eight-legged syringe. Never squeeze them between your fingers to remove them—otherwise, you'll force the bacteria they carry into your body. Instead, remove them by their head, grasping them as close to your skin as possible.

Once the tick is removed, check it closely to make sure the head is still attached. If not, check the bite site. If the head (usually a tiny dark spot, sometimes detectable only with a magnifying glass) can be seen and carefully removed, lift it out with a sterilized needle and then clean the bite area with a cotton swab or tissue soaked with rubbing alcohol. If a tiny portion of the head remains, your skin will shed it during the healing process. And check with your doctor.

ONE MISSING LETTER

A hunter from the east traveled out west to hunt in a national forest. Upon arrival, and after setting up camp, he sent his wife a text. But one little letter missing from his message got him into a ton of trouble. His text read, "Having a wonderful time! Wish you were her."

A FITTING ADMISSION

If the thrill of the kill is the focus and sole meaning of "sport hunting," then there is no moral justification for it. Killing animals for sustenance and survival is, ultimately, the only morally good reason to hunt. But it must be admitted that the challenge of the hunt and acquiring food in that way is undeniably exhilarating.

SUDDENLY

The *suddenlies* that happen while hunting are often the best part of the hunting story. "*Suddenly* I heard the snap of a twig in the woods," or "*Suddenly* the wind swept through, carrying with it the alarming smell of burning forest," or "*Suddenly*, just a few yards away, the huge, angry bear stood up on its hind legs and roared." With the use of the word *suddenly*, the listener is all ears.

THE REAL GAUGE

The real gauge to tell whether or not a person is a diehard hunter is not in the scouting, shooting, or tracking—it's in the patient, sometimes long and grueling wait for the opportunity to put their skills to the test.

THORNY WISDOM

Having experienced more than my share of rips through my camo and painful marks on my skin that rivaled the swipe of a big bear's clawed paw, I appreciate the wisdom of James R. Lowell, who said, "One thorn of experience is worth a whole wilderness of warning."

A GUN IN THE HAND

I read that a man in Canada robbed a bank using a pistol. He was apprehended, and his gun was impounded. Someone in the police department recognized that the handgun was a rare .45 Colt, manufactured under license by the Ross Rifle Company in Quebec City during World War I. It was one of only one hundred pistols of its type ever made. The man didn't know that he could have walked into any gun shop and sold the collector's item for much more than he had stolen—and he would have avoided the consequences of breaking the law.

In this bad economy, the only difference between me and a pigeon is that a pigeon can still make a deposit on a new hunting rifle.

TIM HANSON

Turkey Tip

There was a time when the six weeks of our state's turkey season in the spring wore me down physically. I would get up before daylight morning after morning to be out when the gobblers were waking up.

While I like hearing the sound of thundering toms at dawn, I decided to limit my enjoyment of that thrill to the first week of the season. After that, I head to turkey territory after breakfast and after getting some work done.

This energy-saving, altered agenda began when I discovered that gobblers get lonely when the hens go to their nests, and they start roaming in search of an accepting girl. If I can get a "love-starved" tom to respond to my hen-calling fakery in the middle of the day, my chances of putting him in the frying pan are greater—and a season of exhaustion is avoided.

Outdoor Poetry

Now there he stands with shining rack, the master of his race,
And I with sharpened steel and bow held sure in perfect place.
The hidden stand among the limbs, I knew he could not see.
Is this the hour I've waited for, his life be given to me?
Just one more step, I spoke in silence, and season will be ended.
The wisdom of his many years, his life has not defended.
Now as he stands, that one step taken, his blood about to spill,
My mind slips back two thousand years to a tree on another hill.
His head hung low, His eyes look tired, to give those men a thrill,
The nails, the spear, like arrows cast, about to close the deal.
And then I saw that Master's eyes turn and look at me,
"You're the master of the morning, what will your choice now be?
What did God do when in His eyes your sin left you alone?"
Then deep inside where no one sees, the thrill of death was gone.
Another time, another day, he and I in another place.
That blood today, it's in my soul, and a chorus, "Amazing Grace."

DON HICKS, "MASTER OF THE MORNING"[9]

Elk hunting runs deep. Not that it's always
fun, because it isn't. It's a contrast in superlatives,
ranging from agony to euphoria, and it will
stretch your sense and your senses to the limit.

DWIGHT SCHUH, *GAME COUNTRY*

The search for a scapegoat is the
easiest of all hunting expeditions.

DWIGHT D. EISENHOWER

Nothing clears a troubled mind
like shooting a bow.

FRED BEAR

CONQUERED

To say that by killing a deer I conquered it would be inaccurate because a deer is not a foe to be defeated. What I conquered was my doubt about whether I could actually outsmart the highly sensitive nose, incredibly keen eyesight, and well-honed disappearing skills the animal possessed.

*The hunting partnership between man and dog
developed thousands of years ago and from it came a
deep bond of affection. I suspect this was the dog's idea.*

Aaron Fraser Pass

---

*When he was young, I told Dale Jr. that hunting and
racing are a lot alike. Holding that steering wheel and
holding that rifle both mean you better be responsible.*

Dale Earnhardt

A DAD'S AIM

If your aim is to spend time with your kids in order to make a positive impact on their lives, then take them hunting. You'll hit the bull's-eye on the "good dad" target every time you do.

A dog is the only thing on earth that loves
you more than he loves himself.

Josh Billings

Everybody needs beauty as well as bread, places to
play in and pray in, where Nature may heal and
cheer and give strength to body and soul alike.

John Muir

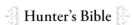 Hunter's Bible

God was with the lad; and he grew, and dwelt
in the wilderness, and became an archer.

Genesis 21:20 kjv

We lose ourselves in the things we love.
We find ourselves there, too.

KRISTIN MARTZ

BOYS WILL BE MEN

Only God knows how many dads have taken a boy to the mountains to hunt big game and, when the adventure ended, brought a man home with them.

A SINGLE ACORN

Next time the fall season arrives, bringing with it a good crop of acorns, take the time to pick one up, put it in your hand, and ponder the incredible fact that in the single acorn you hold is the potential for "the creation of a thousand forests" (Ralph Waldo Emerson).

CHRISTMAS LIST

Mall Santa: "And what do you want for Christmas, little fella?"

Little boy in a camo jacket: "Twenty new mallard decoys, ten boxes of twenty-gauge shells, a single- and a double-reed duck call, thermal underwear, a well-bred Labrador retriever, and a propane heater."

Santa: "That's a lot, young man. Not sure if I can get all of it in my toy bag."

Little boy: "Then add a sixteen-and-a-half foot aluminum john-boat with a seventy-horsepower motor and trailer to the list. It'll carry everything."

THE GREAT VALUE
OF A SINGLE SPARROW

Seeing a sparrow while hunting is a very common occurrence, and the divine truth that the tiny flier represents is rarely considered. Perhaps the next time you see one you'll remember the following verses.

> Are not two sparrows sold for a cent? And yet not one of them will fall to the ground apart from your Father. But the very hairs of your head are all numbered. So do not fear; you are more valuable than many sparrows (Matthew 10:29-31).

This encouraging biblical passage contains a reference to bird hunting: "not one of them [sparrows] will fall to the ground." But there is comfort in the words that follow: "apart from your Father." These verses imply that if God is aware of something as small as a sparrow, we can rest assured that He cares for us. He considers His disciples "more valuable than many sparrows."

I save my sick days because I know come fall
I'm gonna have a bad case of buck fever.

AUTHOR UNKNOWN

*"The best thing about hunting and fishing," the
Old Man said, "is that you don't have to actually
do it to enjoy it. You can go to bed every night
thinking how much fun you had twenty years ago,
and it all comes back as clear as moonlight."*

ROBERT RUARK, *OLD MAN'S BOY GROWS UP*

FAMILIAR TERRITORY

While I thoroughly enjoy hunting new territory, there's
something mysteriously pleasurable about hunting often
on a particular piece of land. I think it's because I feel two emotions simultaneously: comfortable with the familiar scenes, and intensely eager for a sighting. Or maybe it's the advantage of feeling safe that I enjoy. Whatever the reason, I like going back often to familiar woods.

IF THERE WERE MORE OF ME

If there were more of me, I'd keep one here in Tennessee to enjoy life with my beloved wife and family, and I'd send one to be a hunting guide in Montana and another to live on and manage a dude ranch in Idaho. The me I didn't like I'd send to International Falls, Minnesota. It's not that I don't like the people there. They're awesome. I just don't think I could survive their winters. Really, you've gotta have skin like a groundhog to live in that place.

HAWK EARS

It's amazing that a man can't hear his wife talking when she's across the breakfast table from him—but he can hear the faint sound of gobbling two ridges over from where he's standing in the woods.

DIRT, GREASE, AND ROMANCE

There are at least two things I've found to be true about farmers—they love dirt, and they love their trucks. For living proof of this fact, I don't have to look any further than the owner of my favorite farm to hunt.

As I was leaving Joe Goodman's property following a morning deer hunt during bow season, I stopped at his workshop to say hello. While I was there, he asked me to help him write a poem for his wife for their fiftieth anniversary. He handed me a tractor grease–stained piece of paper with a title idea and some lines he had written. When I read them, my heart warmed.

The verses below are evidence that even when Joe tried to be romantic, it came out with dirt, grease, and gasoline. I love it!

Old GMC

Here we are 50 years down the road of life together
I look at you and I can say you're looking better than ever
And I'm amazed that a girl so fine
would want a farm boy like me
Of all the fancy cars on the lot, you
drove away with a GMC
You could've had a Jaguar
You could've had a Cadillac
You could've had a Mercedes-Benz, that's a fact
But you fell in love with a pickup truck
And I'm as happy as I can be
That you chose to ride through this life
In a dusty old GMC
I might have mud on my wheels
From working out there in the fields
But when we go to town and you're siting next to me
You make me shiny as a brand-new Ferrari[10]

THREE HUNTERS,
ONE DECEASED DEER

A preacher, a lawyer, and a real estate agent were walking across a field on their way to their deer stands when a big buck stood up about 50 yards away. All three of the men raised their guns and took a shot. The deer went down where it stood, and the three men ran to the trophy, where they discovered only one bullet had connected.

They got into a heated argument about who had killed the deer, and that's when a game warden showed up. After learning what they were arguing about, the warden offered to take a look at the buck and give his determination. It took only a few seconds for him to render his verdict. "It was definitely the preacher's bullet that killed this buck."

The lawyer and real estate agent asked how he could tell. The officer answered, " 'Cause the bullet went in one ear and out the other."

UNINTENTIONAL LETDOWN

There's a story circulating on the web that may or may not be true—but it illustrates how easily a man can say something wrong and not even know it. It involves a man and his wife who went to a mall to do some Christmas shopping. They got separated from each other, and the wife called him on her cell phone. Miffed by his absence, she asked, "Where are you? We have a lot to do!"

He answered, "Do you remember that jewelry store we visited not long after our wedding, and we saw that necklace you liked, and I said someday I'd get it for you?"

With happy tears filling her eyes, she said, "I do, sweetheart."

He added, "Well, I'm in the gun shop next to it."

WHO'S HAPPIEST TO SEE YOU?

It's been said that if you want to know who is always happiest to see you, put your wife and your beagle in the trunk of your car, close the lid, and drive around for two hours. Open it up, and you'll find out.

HIGHWAY HUNTING HAZARD

Highway hunters are those who drive along looking for deer just because they like to see them. If you're a highway hunter, and you're a married man, be warned. It's a type of hunting that can get you in big trouble, and here's how it can happen.

You're driving through the country, and your wife is with you. There are soybean fields on both sides of the road. It's about 4:30 in the evening, when deer start entering the fields to forage for food. Your wife is talking, but you don't hear her because—that's right—you're hunting. Then she asks a question that you don't actually hear.

"Sweetheart, were you ever in love with someone before we met, and you really wanted to marry them?"

About that time you see a group of deer out in a field, but you're looking right over the bridge of your wife's nose to see them. Then you speak, and she thinks you're looking at her as you reply, "Oh yeah! Nine or ten of 'em—pretty ones too!"

If this happens, be aware that you'll be guilty of driving off the love road and hitting the stupid tree. For the sake of your marriage, don't be a "deer-stracted" driver—at least when your wife is with you.

DEER KINDNESS

When a farmer leaves a few rows of standing corn and residual ears on the ground for deer after harvesting, he is providing an illustration of the instruction God gave farmers in Old Testament times: "When you reap the harvest of your land, moreover, you shall not reap to the very corners of your field nor gather the gleaning of your harvest; you are to leave them for the needy and the alien. I am the LORD your God" (Leviticus 23:22).

THAT EXPLAINS IT

It has been stated countless times that the hunter's favorite Bible verse is Acts 10:13, which says, "There came a voice to him, Rise, Peter; kill, and eat" (KJV). What's not often noted is that Peter heard these words while he was in a trance. This detail can help a wife understand what's happening when her husband gets that faraway look on his face when they're talking and deer season is just a few days away.

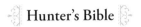

Hunter's Bible

The wolf will dwell with the lamb,
And the leopard will lie down with the young goat,
And the calf and the young lion and the fatling together;
And a little boy will lead them.
Also the cow and the bear will graze,
Their young will lie down together,
And the lion will eat straw like the ox.
The nursing child will play by the hole of the cobra,
And the weaned child will put his hand on the viper's den.
They will not hurt or destroy in all My holy mountain,
For the earth will be full of the knowledge of the LORD
As the waters cover the sea.

ISAIAH 11:6-9

HUNTER'S LOG

Unless we leave behind a written record, the greatest
portion of our life experiences, as well as the lessons
learned from them along the way, is too often
obscured by the passage of time. Consequently, passing
along those valuable insights is threatened.[11]

FEATHER FLOWER

Similar to the goldenrod bloom that shows up in the fall in Tennessee and signals that opening day of deer season is coming, springtime has its bloom that tells turkey hunters that gobbler chasing is just around the corner.

I don't refer to the buttercup that appears in early to mid-March or the colorful blossom on the redbud tree that comes a little later. While both trigger welcome thoughts of the approaching first day of turkey season, they don't compare to what blooms on the tail of a mature male gobbler. I call it the "feather flower." The glory of its spread begins to show with the first hints of warmer weather as February yields to March—and sometimes even earlier if there's a warm wave in our state. When I happen to see the sight of a feather flower glowing in a sunlit field, my trigger finger twitches, and dreams of plucking that bloom fill my head.

An evening [elk] hunt during the last minutes before legal shooting light ends can be magical if you're prepared. Outstanding low-light optics can make the difference between enjoying backstraps for dinner and making do with reheated chili.

JAY HOUSTON

LEAPING LEAF

A single, loosely hanging leaf that swings back and forth in my peripheral vision in the early morning woods where absolutely nothing else is moving can be really annoying. As it sways prankster-like, it can repeatedly fool me into thinking it's time to get ready to face an approaching deer. My excitement skyrockets with the movement, then falls back to earth when I realize it's only a leaf swinging merrily on a hardly detectable thermal. The temptation to shoot the little annoyer and put it out of my misery is strong, but I don't do it for two reasons.

One, the noise of the shot could send the local deer herd running out of the area. Two, the little distracting dangler serves as an illustration of a truth worth remembering and preserving. The leaping leaf is what a Christian looks like in a spiritually dead world. A believer responds to the unseen wind of God's Spirit as He gives joy and peace to the soul, and those who observe that behavior can see that, whether they like it or not, God is alive and is the giver of life.

A WORD TO THE
SEASONED HUNTERS

For all you hunters who are closer to the end of your season of life than the beginning of it and are wondering if you can compete with the young bucks in the woods, don't forget that "old age and treachery will always beat youth and exuberance," as David Mamet said.

THE TIE THAT BINDS

Perhaps the best evidence that hunting is the tie that binds men together is what many call "deer camp." It's the place hunters long to return to year after year, season after season—where lifetime connections are made and felt deeply in the soul. And what happens in places where hunters gather, eat, talk, laugh, eat, disperse to the woods for a while, regather, swap stories, eat some more, and then sleep with dreams of deer encounters doesn't stay there. It all goes home with them and serves as a strong connection between each heart, a tie that even death can't break.

HUNTING PRAYERS

I've been known to whisper a prayer when I catch a glimpse of an approaching deer: "Lord, don't let the wind shift on me," or "Help me stay calm," or "Can you slow down the sunset, please?" I've prayed even more when tracking a wounded deer, especially if the blood trail has turned undetectable.

I'm not really sure if God honors my deer-hunting prayers, but it never hurts to keep the lines of communication open. And when the circumstances turn out favorable, I don't hesitate to thank Him for it. It's all good practice for life outside the woods.

Deer Tip

In the morning, deer will often leave a field where they're feeding and go deep into a thicket to bed. Then in the late afternoon they usually get up and start to meander back to the field, arriving in the openness at—or just after—sunset.

If you opt for evening hunting in the early weeks of archery season, and you place a permanent stand well back in the woods in order to rendezvous with these cautious creatures on their way to browse in the field before sunset, don't forget an important detail. Because the leaves will still be on the trees, it will get dark in the woods well before it does in the field. For that reason, be sure to clear some branches overhead in the area of your stand to let in some extra shooting light.

Rabbit Tip

According to an expert hunting guide and beagle trainer I've hunted with on more than one occasion, a cottontail has a trait that is not in his favor but bodes well for the hunter. Six times out of ten, after being jumped and chased by beagles, a rabbit will circle around and come right back to where they were first jumped.

This is why it's better to stay put at the jump spot, wait, and listen carefully to the bark of the dogs. Their approaching sound will tell you that it's time to watch closely for the rabbit, which will be moving fast several yards ahead of the dogs. That's when you need to do two things. First and foremost, look around and make sure no other hunter is in range. Second, prepare to slide the gun safety to the firing position so you can take a shot—or two, or three.

BEAGLE MUSIC

Hunter to beagle trainer and rabbit-hunting guide: "Why did you bring fourteen dogs?"

Guide (with a huge smile): "Well…a trio singing at church is nice, but man, when that choir sings!"

⇥ Outdoor Poetry ⇤

Morning sun on a mountain snow
Paints the world a golden glow
Bluebird singing in a meadow green
Feeling the freedom in his wings

These are...
Moments of heaven
Here on the earth
No way to measure what they are worth
Praise to the Father
For the joy He has given
To be touched now and then
By moments of heaven
A gentle breeze in a cottonwood's shade
Cools the skin on a July day
Children laughing, playing in the park
Not a single worry in their hearts

Family table, breaking bread
Love and peace in every word that's said
Someone's missing, they've been gone too long
Look down the road, see them coming home

These are...
Moments of heaven
Here on the earth
No way to measure what they are worth
Praise to the Father
For the joy He has given
To be touched now and then
By moments of heaven[12]

IT'S THE DOE, DUDE

Tom Malouf of Malouf Trophy Whitetails in Wills Point, Texas, reported, "Everything changed when I discovered through years of research that the key to growing trophy bucks is not related so much to the genes in the fathers but those in the mother."

Applying this discovery to my own life, I've realized that being married to Annie explains why our only begotten "buck" is so awesome.

Elk Tip

When you're getting ready for the challenge of pursuing the mighty elk in a mountainous western state, keep in mind these words from expert elk hunter and guide Jay Houston: "You will never experience excellence as long as you settle for mediocre."

Jay has been with hunters who weren't ready for the elk test—and the disappointment left them devastated. So let Jay's urging haunt you in the best of ways as you train your legs and lungs for the long and strenuous climbs—and as you repeatedly draw your bow or aim your rifle in preparation for the moment when that wall-hanger bull is standing broadside in range.

THE RIGHT QUESTION

To the wife of a hunter who wishes he would talk more, I offer this tip: Ask him the right question. When he gets home from the woods, meet him with, "See anything?" Just be prepared to listen—until you pass out.

DON'T EVEN ASK

To save your marriage and salvage your hunting rights, I recommend the following (from experience): Never ask if it's okay to go to the woods with your soon-to-be son-in-law on the morning of the day your daughter will marry him. Even if you promise that you'll be back in time for the ceremony, it won't work. You might hear these chilling words in response: "If you go to the woods that day, you'll *never* get out of the woods!"

MARRIAGE ADVICE FOR HUNTERS

It's always smart for a husband to earn his hunting time. This can be accomplished, for example, by asking what needs to be done around the house (and doing it without complaining), or by keeping small children for a few hours while their mother gets a break. Sitting in a deer stand or a turkey or duck blind free of guilt just makes the hunt even sweeter.

PUT HER FIRST

For the sake of keeping a marriage strong, I'm a proponent of the husband getting his wife's full support for a costly, guided hunt. To accomplish that goal, sometimes it helps to convince her of how the hunt will benefit her life.

In my case, for example, I had an opportunity to go to Montana for a spring black bear hunt. With all the sincerity I could muster, I said, "Babe, I really need to go out west and kill a big black bear." She asked why. I pointed to the beautiful flower garden she had created in our backyard and said, " 'Cause I'm sure that bear is gonna migrate to Tennessee and get in your garden and destroy it."

It all worked out. The new sunroom she negotiated for in lieu of the cost of the bear hunt looks great, and I'm still married.

VALEN-"TIMES" DAY

If you're a husband and a deer hunter, too, you should know that Valentine's Day is very well placed on the calendar. Six weeks after your poor handling of Christmas is about the time your wife is starting to get over what a Scrooge you were. That's when your apology accompanied by a gift of flowers, a thoughtful card, and a dinner date might be accepted—along with the news that the big buck with those ten-inch brow tines you got during deer season is at the taxidermy shop. Timing is everything!

TWO VALENTINE'S DAY MESSAGE IDEAS

To my fellow hunters who are married, I have two ideas for Valentine's Day messages you can give your sweetheart. If you want to be brief and to the point you can try this: "You're just like my .30-30…a joy to hold."

If you feel like you need to say more, you're welcome to copy the following song lyrics I wrote for my wife. I refer to this as my "Valentune." I must confess that it went over much better than option one.

That's What I Get

I had no way of knowing
Where loving you would lead
Such a risky thing to do
Still I said, "Will you marry me?"
And you did
I was glad
And what did I get for that?

Somebody's hand to hold in mine
Somebody's faith to help me through the hard times
Somebody's trust that I'll always be true
That's what I get for loving you

Well, all at once it's been years ago
But I think about that day now and then
When I said I'd love you till I die
Would I do it all again?
Yes, I would
That's a fact
'Cause now I know what I'd get for that

Somebody's smile when I come home
Somebody's hope when it seems my hope is gone
Somebody praying for the work I do
That's what I get for loving you

Somebody's arms to keep me warm
Somebody's mercy that forgives me when I'm wrong
Somebody's peace when the world has come unglued
That's what I get for loving you[13]

Successful elk hunters not only stay at it longer; they are willing
to go farther. They are willing to venture into that unexplored
*territory…*hic sunt dracones*. They are prepared mentally*
and physically to move across one drainage into the next, and
the next, and the next if that is what it takes. Elk are where
we find them, which is rarely where we want them to be.

JAY HOUSTON

The difference between the hunter and the hunted
is that the former can allow himself a mistake.

JORGE WAGENSBERG

Outdoor Poetry

There is a pleasure in the pathless woods,
There is a rapture on the lonely shore,
There is society, where none intrudes,
By the deep Sea, and music in its roar:
I love not Man the less, but Nature more.

LORD BYRON

A FISHERMAN ON AGING

When we talked about feeling the effects of aging, my friend and expert fisherman Jim Grenz, who has seen a lot of sunsets while in his boat off the coast of Canada, said, "My sun is not setting quite yet, but it's well into the western sky."

Hunter's Hint

Giving an often-used deer stand location a name can help friends know each other's whereabouts. It can also contribute to a safer hunt. To illustrate, as my buddy and I are about to leave the truck for a morning hunt he might say, "I'm going to *the Gate Stand*. And you?" I might answer, "I'll be at *the Clump*." With that short exchange, we know exactly where not to aim our rifles.

SUREFIRE ACTION STARTERS

If you're not seeing anything while in the deer stand, take one of the following steps, and something will likely show up. Each one of these options has worked fabulously for me.

- Take out your cell phone and check your email.

- Dig around in your daypack for a snack.

- Open your thermos.

- Stand up to stretch.

- Respond to your bladder calling.

- Take an unintentional nap.

- Retrieve a book you brought along to read.

- Start gathering your gear to leave.

DOGS AND DEER

When a deer hunter in a stand hears the distant sound of an approaching, barking dog, they know it can mean one of two things. Either the hunt is over and it's time to pack up and head home, or—preferably—there are deer heading your way and the action is about to begin.

SNAP

The anger-induced snap of my mother's fingers that I heard when I was a kid is similar to the distinct snap of a twig under a deer's hoof that I hear these days when I'm hunting. The emotions those sounds have generated, however, are not at all the same. The former caused unwanted fear and dread; the latter causes anticipation and welcome excitement. Both are unforgettable.

✦ Deer Tip ✦

To keep your camo as free as possible from odors that might alert the wary nose of a deer, gather freshly fallen leaves from trees common to your area and place them in large plastic, scentless trash bags along with your camo. Include your hat, face mask, tops, bottoms or overalls, gloves, and socks. After each hunt place your entire set of camo in the bag until the next outing.

A TRUTH WE CAN LIVE WITH

Hunters who've had a long and grueling search for a wounded animal that yielded no recovery will sometimes sigh and say something like, "Well, the coyotes have to eat too." Why would any of us settle on that conclusion? It's because an animal that may be suffering due to a failed shot is a sad thought that's very hard to handle. Predators eating the wounded animal is not the preferred outcome by any means—but it's a truth hunters can live with.

THEN AND NOW

Ever since I started hunting turkeys several decades ago, I've been the type who depends on hearing the big boys gobble to locate their whereabouts. If I stop to listen and too much time passes before I hear one thunder, I'm on the move.

As a younger man, when it was time to head to the next ridge I would say, "If their gobblin' is done, I'm on the run," and bound away like a gazelle to find some vocal birds. I'm older now, but nothing has changed in regard to my impatient approach to chasing turkeys—except for one thing. Due to the fact that I'm not as agile as I once was, when I decide to go mobile I say, "If they ain't talkin', I'm walkin'."

"AT LEAST I KNOW…"

No matter what happens during a hunt, there's always something positive to remember about it. For example, if I strategize carefully and choose what I think is the right stand location for the conditions, but I still leave the woods empty-handed, I can say, "At least I know where I shouldn't have been."

SEASONED NAVIGATORS

You know you're a well-seasoned, experienced deer hunter when you're navigating through a new patch of woods and, without realizing it at first, you end up following a deer trail. And when you do realize it, you intentionally step several feet to the side of the path so you don't leave your scent on the ground and on the foliage that lines the trail.

"HUNTIN' IN THE RAIN"

One of my favorite times to hunt deer is during a rainfall. The advantages are too good to pass up, such as the water-soaked leaves, soft and quiet under my boots, and the noise of the raindrops hitting the ground, covering the sound of a twig I might inadvertently break. In the rain my tactics turn to still-hunting—that is, moving slowly through the woods, stepping from tree to tree, waiting for a few minutes at each stop, and scanning the woods for deer that may be waiting out the downpour. More than once I've enjoyed these unique conditions that many hunters avoid, and it has yielded some success.

LONG-SUFFERING

Hunters can be listed among those who illustrate the meaning of a word that has biblical roots but is rarely used today: *long-suffering*. In the Old Testament, the ancient words translated as "long-suffering" mean "long of nose," which refers to the heavy breathing that controlled anger can generate. If a person is long-suffering, then they are intentionally showing a great deal of patience and endurance even though it isn't easy.[14]

So when a hunter willingly sits for hours in a stand in the bitter cold with a rifle or faces an annoying, prolonged endurance of a relentless swarm of gnats in the early weeks of archery season, it can be said that he or she is long-suffering. The benefit comes when a difficult situation in life outside of the woods demands a lot of patience. In those times, it doesn't take a lot of explaining for a hunter to know how to be long-suffering.

MY ANNIE (OAKLEY)

After my wife took the class required for getting Tennessee's handgun carry permit, she came home with a wide smile on her face. With a tone of pride she announced that not only had she passed the written exam, but she also had impressed the instructor with a perfect score at the shooting range using her six-shot, .38 caliber revolver. I smiled back and said with humility, "Babe, I feel safer—and more obedient!" I wasn't kidding.

THE KEY TO ENJOYMENT

I try not to put a lot of pressure on myself when I hunt. I approach hunting sort of like I do golfing. I leave the house with high hopes and low expectations. Each activity is more enjoyable that way.

MOUNTAINEER METHODS

A hunter from the Mountain State (West Virginia) and my nephew by marriage, Jason Click, bagged one of the most impressive bucks I've ever seen. I asked him to email me a few tips that have yielded success for him. I thought I'd heard it all, but his reply proved to me that you really can teach an old hunter new tricks.

1. *When hunting with another hunter or in a group, I always let them be the first to pick where they want to hunt on the property. I always take the "less desirable" spot because deer seem to know where the usual pressure is and often will head to the less desirable area.*

2. *During archery season, if I bump into a deer on the way to a stand early in the morning while it's still dark, I use my grunt call as I walk. Immediately after getting in my stand, I use the grunt call again. If the deer I bumped didn't wind me, there's a good chance they could think*

Jason's Buck   SC

it was a buck that walked through instead of a hunter. As soon as shooting light comes up, I use the grunt call again. If there was a buck among the deer that were bumped while walking in, he may come back to explore or to confront the intruder. This tactic is what I used when I took my record-book buck—my biggest so far.

3. *During archery season I will take an arrow out of my quiver and lightly tap it against my bow limb. It can sound like the tinkling of antlers that is made by bucks when they spar. Along with the arrow tapping, I use my grunt call. I've taken some bucks with this method.*

4. *Because bucks are very vocal during the rut, I use the grunt call a lot during that part of the season.*

5. *I admit it sounds strange, but I include this tip—I purchase a box of unscented tampons and put my Tink's Number 69 scent attractant on them. The string is perfect for tying to a tree limb below my stand. The only drawback is the Walmart checkout experience.*

When I opened Jason's email, which came with an attached photo of his record-book buck, I confess that my first thought was, *There's not a jealous bone in my body!*

⚜ Deer Tip ⚜

I used to be a real stickler about not "tinkling" on the ground while in a deer stand. To avoid what I believed was a mistake that could alert the nose of a deer, I usually carried a glass bottle in my daypack to use for relieving my bladder. (I chose glass because a warming plastic bottle can pop like a bursting balloon.)

Not anymore. I eliminated the glass latrine after I heard a very seasoned and successful deer hunter say that, in his opinion, urine is urine. I was nervous about abandoning my bottle policy, but I found that my old friend was right. I've watched deer walk right by my leafy latrine beneath my stand. I will admit, however, if I've had asparagus before the hunt, the glass bottle goes with me. Better to be safe than smelly.

DEER VERSUS TURKEY

There are two good reasons why turkey hunting is more senior friendly than deer hunting. One, turkey hunting doesn't require an aging body to endure long, motionless sits. Getting up and moving around to call and locate a gobbler is a welcome relief to easily stiffened joints and muscles. Second, when it comes to getting a critter back to the truck, a seasoned hunter whose strength may not be what it once was appreciates the difference between an easily toted 20-pound turkey and a backbreaking, heart-threatening 150-pound deer.

AN OUTSIDER SPEAKS

During a conversation with a nonhunter I was offered a suggestion that is worth consideration. As I remember it, the fellow said, "I'm not a hunter, and I don't have anything against it, but I've watched a few hunting shows with family members who hunt—and there's something that's often said on camera after the kill that is really confusing. I suspect that serious anti-hunting types hear it, and it makes their blood boil. As the hunter pats and rubs the deer, they do commentary and usually say, 'What a beautiful buck!'

"My reaction is likely the same as the anti's. I think, *Beautiful? Say what? If you think it's beautiful, then why did you kill it? Dead ain't pretty!* For the sake of avoiding the visual and verbal contrast, it seems to me that using words like *impressive* or *awesome* as they grin and stroke the animal's lifeless body would be more appropriate—anything but beautiful. Just saying..."

"FALL" HUNTING HURTS

There's *fall hunting*, and then there's *hunting fall*. The former is enjoyable, while the latter can kill. I've experienced both, but thankfully I've only fallen from a tree stand once. After experiencing the pain of a hunting fall, I searched for a way not to repeat such a season-ending disaster.

I'm happy to say that I found it. Using this innovative device, I can guarantee that I'll never fall from a tree stand again. It's called…a three-legged stool. It's foldable, portable, and sits on the ground, allowing me to avoid another potentially deadly tumble from an elevated stand. For it to work it must be used exclusively—but I'm not there yet.

Hunter's Bible

Since the creation of the world His invisible attributes, His eternal power and divine nature, have been clearly seen, being understood through what has been made, so that they are without excuse.

ROMANS 1:20

⚮ Deer Tip ⚮

I've always been hesitant to use a flashlight in the pre-dawn hours while going to a deer stand because a flashlight is not a "flash" at all. Instead, what we call a flashlight is actually a constantly glowing lamp. Surely the sight of a beam that appears to be bouncing as it moves can spook the deer.

To avoid that possibility, I turn my flashlight into what its name implies—flashes of light. When I come to a place in the woods where I'm not sure of what's ahead, I turn the light on and off and use the momentary bursts of light to find my way. Why? Deer are used to seeing flashes of light from occasional lightning storms, as well as the headlights from passing vehicles. It's just one more small way to outwit the wily eyes and minds of the local herd.

BACK TO THE WOODS

O n a chilly late-December morning before daylight, my son, Nathan, and I arrived at a farm to hunt deer. After dressing at the truck and loading our rifles, I directed Nate to a stand I called "the Two Man," located at the edge of a large patch of woods next to a huge soybean field. He planned to stay all day for a reason I deeply appreciated. It was his first time to hunt an entire day in at least 15 years. He was so determined and excited to get to spend every daylight hour in the stand that he passed on taking a doe that bedded down just a few yards from his stand not long after sunrise.

The day ended without a shot fired, but Nate couldn't have been more pleased to have had the chance to hunt from dawn to dusk—and I couldn't have been more pleased that it was something he wanted to do. I'll explain why, beginning with some personal history.

If someone were to ask me which decade of my life I'd consider the most memorable, I would have to say it was my forties. Of course, all the decades have been great, but looking back through my journey there are a few things about my forties that I especially enjoyed.

Unlike my thirties, which were chock-full of the time-consuming challenges of growing babies into toddlers and working to establish a business, the forties weren't as slammed. By then I had been married long enough that Annie and I had become an effective team as parents and co-laborers. Also, we had reached a level of income that allowed us to maintain our budget and have some expendable cash. By my forties our children were into their early teens, and their increasing ability to care for themselves meant more time for me to do things I had put on the back burner. One of those activities was my favorite of all—hunting.

When I got back to this pastime, I didn't abandon our son to do so. Instead, I introduced him to the "fair chase," and we had some great times chasing squirrels and rabbits in West Virginia, deer in Tennessee and the Dakotas, and even elk in Montana. Nathan's skill as a hunter developed quickly, and he thoroughly enjoyed the adventures.

Eventually, however, Nate's life went the way mine did when my hunting days went dark around 20 years old. He went to college, met his wife while there, and then they had their own children. The cares of life that come with the thirties overcame his time to hunt.

Through his third decade Nate may have hunted one day annually in some of the years and none in others. He often talked about going hunting again, but as a helpful husband, a dad of three kids, and a producer in the music business (Grammy-winning producer, I might brag…er, add)—among other life responsibilities—he simply didn't have any extra free time. But then he entered his forties, and I watched history repeat itself in his journey.

Hungry to head to the woods with some level of regularity again, he announced to me that he had gone to a sporting-goods store and purchased camo coveralls, boots, blaze-orange vests, and other gear. I had done the same thing around my fortieth birthday, and I knew why he had decided to round up some equipment. His schedule had opened up. It all looked so familiar.

I've wondered how many other guys have followed a similar path on the trail of time, one that took them away from hunting for a long while and then back to it. I suspect there are many—and I may be wrong, but my guess is that those who are in that category are men who have taken their roles as husband and dad seriously enough to willingly put their outdoor fun on hold during the most demanding time of their lives. Simply put, they know that succeeding at family life is a lot more important than succeeding in the deer stand.

The beginning of Nathan's reentry into the woods was a thrill to observe. Not only was it interesting to watch my story repeat itself, but it was also satisfying to know that an activity I had introduced him to many years ago was something so enjoyable and meaningful to him that he wanted to get back to it. Another reason I was thrilled is that he has two young boys who will benefit by his return to the outdoors. They're already "speaking the language."

Within a few days following that first all-day hunt I mentioned earlier, Nate called and said he wanted to go back to the "Two Man" stand and give it another try. I was more than happy to accompany him. We parted ways at the truck as we had done previously, and I headed to another part of the farm to hunt—and wait.

When I took my seat in my stand, I whispered a prayer for my son that he'd be rewarded for the sacrifice he had made for the sake of his family. It's hard to explain how thankful I was when, around 6:55 a.m., I heard the distant blast of a rifle. My heart leaped with hope that the sound was the report of Nate's .30-30

Marlin (the rifle he had used to get his first deer 25 years earlier). Thirty seconds later my hope was realized when I got a text that is forever etched in my memory: "Got him!"

With a single shot, my deserving son—whose hunting days had been necessarily few for so long—had been blessed with an impressive eight-point Tennessee buck. We were both happy he had come back to the woods.

A REVERSAL OF ROLES

Like all animals, deer are incapable of growing their own food for sustenance. Consequently, they must browse for that which nature provides. Hunters are well aware of this fact and use it to their advantage in at least two ways:

- setting up their stands next to natural food sources, such as nut- and fruit-bearing trees and open meadows

- "assisting" nature through creating deer-attracting food plots and then placing their well-hidden stands along routes that lead to them

If this entire scenario were reversed and humans were hunted by deer, the deer would set up their hideouts near grocery stores and restaurants. It's sobering to think that if this were the case, how quickly and easily their tags would be filled.

HEART-WRENCHING WORDS

A victim of Alzheimer's who was hunting with his son made one of the most heart-wrenching statements I've ever heard. After downing a deer, he turned to his son and said,

"The first deer I got was exciting…but there's nothing like the last one."

WHAT IF?

What if hunters approached going to church like going to the woods on opening day of deer season? They'd willingly and excitedly bound out of bed at the sound of the alarm, show up at the front door of the sanctuary well before daylight, be dressed in clothes very fitting for the environment without a hint of offensive odor, and happily sit for hours in the pew listening intently, dreading the moment it was time to leave and go home. Then after dismissal they'd stand and talk for an hour or two with their fellow churchgoers about how the morning went, what they saw in the sermon, and how much they looked forward to going to church again.

THE COST FOR CROW

I've seen movies that include a scene where someone fires a gun and suddenly, for a few seconds, the sound goes quiet to depict the character's instantaneous loss of hearing. Whenever I see this cinematic portrayal, I'm immediately taken back to my early teens.

At the edge of a patch of woods on a farm in West Virginia, I hunted crows with a friend. We crouched shoulder to shoulder, waiting on some birds to come in close enough for a shot. When they did, before I could raise my single-shot 20-gauge, my friend raised his double-barrel 12-gauge, took quick aim, and pulled both triggers simultaneously—a mere foot or two from my head.

As the world around me went completely still, I realized I was paying a heavy cost for the crow that was flopping on the ground in front of us. I wasn't sure if I'd ever hear again. But slowly the fader in my body's audio board began to slide upward, and after about ten minutes my hearing seemed to be back to normal.

Today I'm keenly aware of the need for ear protection, and I highly recommend it to all gun handlers who will—and can—listen.

IF DEER COULD TALK

If there's one thing I could tell every young deer hunter who chooses to go the woods with a bow and a quiver of arrows, it would be the following song lyrics, written as if the message were delivered by the deer.

Be Ready

The crown of creation—it's you; it's not me
I'm here for another reason; I was born to be
A coat for your shoulders in the cold and the rain
And the life in my flesh, it will feed you I know
So I'm sure you will come with your arrow and bow
But don't forget, I can feel pain

So this one thing I ask of you
This one thing I beg you to do
Be ready, practice, learn from the masters
So that on that day when it's me you come after
Your arrow will fly straight and true
And I will find mercy when it passes through
Like falling asleep in the midmorning sun
If your shot is certain, it's how the end will come for me
Be ready when you come for me[15]

DRUMMING WHILE DRIVING

I took my son and his friend to a neighboring state to hunt deer at the invitation of a gentleman who was a member of the local wildlife management agency. We entered the woods before daylight, and he led each of us to different stands on the property. Around 9:00 a.m. we regrouped, and the collective report of no deer sightings prompted me to suggest to our host that he and I try moving the deer that might be bedded down by putting on a drive. My goal was to help our young hunters get a shot. He agreed, but I detected some reservations in his demeanor about the idea.

We placed the two shooters in stands and began the drive. I was on one side of the hill, and he was on the other. As we started up the wide hollow, I was confident that the leaves crunching under our boots would create plenty of noise to push the deer by the boys. Not so for our host. I could hear him talking, sometimes humming, and pounding two sticks together as he moved through the timber.

While I walked along and listened to his muffled voice and the rhythmic tapping of the sticks, I wondered if he was attempting not only to wake the whitetails but, more important, to help the boys avoid making the dreaded error of mistaking him for a deer. Was it a matter of life and death to him?

When we regrouped, I asked him about his choice of vocalizing and drumming during the drive. I learned that in his years of being with the agency, he had seen too many tragedies involving younger and inexperienced hunters who had mistaken humans for deer. He was not about to become part of those statistics.

His tactic sure was effective that day. Not only did my son and his friend leave the woods with no regrets, but our host also made it home alive. His method is an idea worth passing on to all who drive for others—no matter their age.

IF YOU'RE LOST

You probably already know this, but in a time of panic you might forget it. If you're lost in the woods or the mountains, and you have a smartphone with a map app or GPS on it—along with cell service—don't despair. Make sure your location feature is on, open the map or GPS app, and watch for the blinking dot that tells you where you are. If you have no signal where you are, you might need to climb higher. If there is no available signal, or if you don't have access to a GPS, start yelling.

WHY FISHERMEN?

Among the twelve disciples Jesus chose, four were fishermen. Could it be that Christ chose them to be "fishers of men" (Matthew 4:19) because He knew they'd easily understand and appreciate the key to successful fishing? That is, in order to catch (both fish and converts) you must first cast (a net or the gospel). Also, perhaps Jesus chose fishermen because He knew they were willing to work hard, keep long hours, and move to new waters when necessary—all for the sake of the sweet reward of fish in the boat.

BACK TO THE POSITIVE

When I'm heading to a stand on foot before daylight and I jump deer in the dark, it's always a negative. But I can get back to the positive quickly when I remember that there are other deer in the area that I didn't jump—and they don't know I'm there.

A WORD TO THE UNWISE

Never ever—I repeat, *never ever*—use the scope on your gun to identify a person. It's dangerous and just plain stupid. I speak from the chilling experience of having looked through my binoculars at a hunter who was looking at me—through his scope.

A WORLD MADE
BETTER BY HUNTERS

Hunting can feed mankind in more ways than one. Besides the life-sustaining food source of meat taken from the wild, the lessons learned while in the outdoors about virtues such as patience and endurance can plant, nourish, and strengthen good character in a person. The result of these physical and ethical benefits of hunting is stronger and more trustworthy people who can make the world a better place to live.

SLIP AWAY

Most hunters will agree that one of the most important benefits of being outdoors is the mental and emotional rest it offers. Those who are going full bore every day in an effort to take care of others can grow weary in doing well. While such work is commendable, the problem comes when people won't admit that they need a break, and exhaustion weakens or even sickens the body.

We sometimes learn the hard way that, whether we want to or not, we will rest. Either we break or we have to take a break. Even Jesus knew this to be true. The proof of it is in Luke 5:16. Jesus was constantly pressed by the crowds that followed Him and looked to Him to meet their needs, and He "would often slip away to the wilderness and pray."

As far as I'm concerned, if Jesus needed to head to a quiet place from time to time, then I do too. The following song I wrote with Carter Bentley speaks to this need.

Nearly Sixty-Nine

He said, "I'm nearly sixty-nine
I'm on the backside of my time
In the mirror what I see
Lookin' back at me
Is a man who's tired and weary to the bone
Feels like I've spent my years
Runnin' in high gear
So much on my list
Can't keep it up like this
Gotta get some rest, then I'll press on

"I'm gonna shut it all down
Get away from town
Take my tent, take my truck
Watch the sun coming up
Take a rod and take a reel
Find a lake and just be still
And make some plans to have no plans at all
Gotta rest my weary soul for a while…then I'll press on"

I was there on the day
He packed up to drive away
He had a photograph
Of his bride on the dash
He's missed her so bad since she's been gone
He was counting on the road
To help lighten up his load
Before we said goodbye
He looked me in the eye
And he said, "Son, I'll be back, then I'll press on

"I'm gonna shut it all down
Get away from town
Take my tent, take my truck
Watch the sun coming up
Take my Gibson, take some tunes
Sing to her beyond the moon
Take the Word and take a prayer
Climb a hill and meet God there
And make some plans to have no plans at all
Gotta rest my weary soul for a while…then I'll press on"[16]

NOT ALONE

Sometimes when I settle into a deer stand in the pre-dawn darkness and begin the wait for first light, I wonder how many other hunters are doing the exact same thing at that very moment. Their number is unknown to me, but no matter how many there are, I feel a connection to each one—a shared sense of anticipation for the challenge that sunrise can bring us.

But it's not just my contemporaries to whom I feel linked. I also sense a connection to those who have preceded me in the woods, even back to ancient times. As I imagine what past hunting experiences were like with handmade bows and arrows, spears, traps, and other weapons, I can't help but think that, out of necessity, their skills as hunters were much more developed than mine.

Though that may be true, I am no less linked to my hunting ancestors. I feel their presence at times, and I smile inside when I realize that I might be by myself in a deer stand on a quiet morning, but in no way am I alone.

BOYS LIKE BEN

While hunting for hogs in the area around the Malouf white-tail ranch in Texas, I heard the inspiring story of a young deer hunter named Ben. What he accomplished at the age of ten is simply amazing—not because of the size of the buck he tagged, but because of what he endured in order to do so.

With his focus on one particularly well-antlered deer that roamed the huge territory, Ben climbed into a specific stand an astounding 25 times, with each vigil lasting for hours. Hunt after hunt ended without a shot being fired, and he'd reluctantly dismount and head home tired and disappointed. But with the encouragement and guidance of his woods-wise and lovingly attentive grandfather, Alan, Ben managed to dig deep into his well of youthful determination and commit to going back and trying again.

As the legal season for deer hunting wound down, the young-ster's concern that the year would end without success made him feel anxious. But as much as he worried, he grew that much more determined to close the deal on the big buck. Even with such an uncommon level of stick-to-itiveness for someone his age, his rifle bore remained cold and clean—that is, until the final day of the season.

The ranch owner, Tom Malouf, decided to step in and help Ben try to locate the wary buck by driving him around the prop-erty on his ATV. The ride was quiet except for the soft puttering of the engine as they moved along and scanned the woods and fields.

Finally, Tom cut the engine and, in a low but excited whisper, said the words Ben wanted to hear: "There he is!"

They spotted the buck inside a huge patch of timber, but Ben's chance for a shot was short lived. The smart trophy wheeled on its back hooves, took off, and escaped their view. Tom knew the farm well, so he fired up the ATV and headed to another vantage point.

One more time, as the sun was setting, the prize that Ben longed to earn was seen standing broadside about 100 yards away. Tom started to coach Ben through the shot process and remind him to aim at the buck's shoulder. However, before he could say three words the ear-busting blast of Ben's rifle reported to everyone hunting within two miles that a bullet was on the fly.

Tom shook his head in amazement as he watched the buck crumple to the ground right where it stood. Sensing that there would be no need for following a blood trail, Ben quickly hightailed it to the deer. When Tom arrived at the side of the very happy young hunter and his trophy, he looked the deer over and couldn't believe that Ben had shot the buck at the base of its neck.

Tom asked why Ben had taken a neck shot instead of targeting the shoulder. Ben's response made Tom grin big that day, and he smiled again as he repeated it to me. "Ben looked up at me, wide eyed and still out of breath, and said, 'I shot him in the neck 'cause I wanted to make sure he didn't get away!' "

Tom noted that of all the hunts that have happened on his ranch, Ben's adventure remains on the short list of the greats. He couldn't believe how dedicated such a young boy was to his mission. When Tom told me the story, I offered my prediction of what's likely ahead for Ben.

"Tom, I've hunted with a boy like Ben, and my guess is that because he's self-motivated and relentless in his pursuit of a goal like bagging that buck, he will excel and be a leader at whatever he does. It takes a strong core character to do what he did, and not every kid is built that way. His drive *will be* rewarded with success in other areas of his life, not just in hunting—and people around him will benefit by it."

The reason I could say this is because I watched a boy I know sit in a stand for hours on end to get a whitetail. I saw him hunt hard and long for rabbits without a hint of complaint about the bitter cold that gnawed mercilessly at his nose, toes, and fingers. And I was there to observe him fight through the burning of the muscles in his legs as he trekked up tall, steep mountainsides in the west in pursuit of elk and mule deer. Today that boy has huge racks of antlers and skillfully stuffed critters as proof that his persistence paid off.

That same boy carried his go-get-'em attitude into his teens, college years, and adulthood. He is now a husband and dad. At every point along the way he has excelled because he hasn't settled when it comes to "tagging the trophy." Eventually he made it to the top of the heap in his business, which is producing music. I was privileged to see him on TV the night he was handed a Grammy Award for Album of the Year as a producer.

Who is that kid? You've probably guessed by now that he's my son. I am profoundly proud of him—and I'm very quick, as you can tell, to brag on him. Based on what I've seen from Nathan, whose tenacious fortitude was nurtured and made stronger by being a hunter, I stand firm on my prediction about a young Texan named Ben. Simply put, boys like Ben make great men.

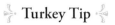 Turkey Tip

Don't call loud,
Don't call much,
Stroke the slate
With a tender touch.
Do it now
And do it then,
Wait a while,
Call again.
Hold to the truth
That less is more,
And you'll enjoy
A tasty reward.

BEAUTY AND DANGER

The wolf and the mountain lion are proof that sometimes beauty and danger exist in the same creature. This is true for people too. If the mighty man Samson would have understood this reality, maybe he would have avoided Delilah (see Judges 16).

⚜ Hunter's Hint ⚜

I f you haul an antlered kill back to camp or your vehicle with a four-wheeler, be sure to mount the animal on the frame so that the antler tips are facing backward. This could prevent you from getting impaled if you have to go up a steep hill and inadvertently flip the machine, causing you to fall backward.

TELL ME SOMETHING
I DIDN'T KNOW

I agree with my friend's opinion about hunting videos. He said, "I can't tell you how many times I've watched a hunter take an animal on camera, then after they find their kill they sit next to it and retell in detail what I just saw—as if my memory is no longer than that of a goldfish. I wish instead they'd offer some insight regarding how they managed to outsmart the animal they downed so I could hear and learn something I didn't know."

A LEGACY OF GENEROSITY

I was on my way to the home of a family of ten to deliver a freshly processed, cost-free doe when a thought crossed my mind relating to my late father. *This is something Dad would do.* More than once I went along with him as he took store-bought food to people who needed it, leaving them wiping tears of gratitude from their eyes. It was especially heartwarming to watch the hungry kids look wide eyed at the bags of groceries on their table.

The only difference between what I delivered that day and what Dad had once delivered was what was in the bags. Dad was not a hunter and was never interested in it, so he wouldn't have hauled a load of venison—but one thing that moved him to be generous was the same thing that motivated me. He just did what his very giving dad would have done.

As the owner of Chapman's Market on the main road through the small town of Chapmanville, West Virginia, my grandpa, George S. Chapman, served his neighbors and folks from the surrounding communities through his grocery business. When I say "served," I mean just that. Because so many of his regular customers were on limited income, Grandpa allowed them to have a running tab at his store.

I remember well the stacks of hand-sized receipt booklets around the cash register, each one with a different name written at the top. The person would shop and take the items to the counter, and Grandpa would list the items on their pad. He'd take whatever amount the customer could pay and give them the top white receipt with the adjusted total. Then they'd be on their way, leaving behind an assumed promise to cover the entire amount in due time.

Of course, not everyone kept their promise to Grandpa. Through the years I heard my dad, aunts, and uncles say that if Grandpa had been paid in full what he was owed, he would have been an extremely wealthy man in those times. But Grandpa's heart was big enough that he gave much grace to the needy who couldn't pay and forgiveness to those who could but wouldn't. The truth is, he was indeed a rich man—rich in compassion.

My grandfather's example of a giving soul was passed on to my dad, who in turn passed it on to me. It was pure joy for me to deliver free deer meat to another family. In turn, I hope my son and daughter will want to be generous to others.

Something My Dad Would Do

They were broke down on the highway
Had two little kids in the back seat
I thought about driving on by
But I couldn't get past the memory
Of being in the car with my father
A long time ago
When he saw a family in need of help
He pulled off the road
So I did too
It's something my dad would do

I get my chances now and then
To live life just like him
To help somebody with a heavy load
And get 'em back out on the road
And lend a hand
Do what I can
To be a man
The light of the Lord can shine through
It's just something my dad would do

I met her at the checkout
She was buying for her son near the front lines
I gave a thank-you smile and started to leave
But the moment took me back in time
To that day at that same old store
In my teenage years
I saw my father pay a stranger's bill
And left them standing there in tears
So I did too
It's something my dad would do

Now I can't help but wonder
Will there come a day
When a child of mine will think of me
And have a reason to say…

"I get my chances now and then
To live life just like him
To help somebody with a heavy load
And get 'em back out on the road
And lend a hand
Do what I can
To be a man
The light of the Lord can shine through
It's just something my dad would do"[17]

TREE LOVER

It's interesting how many types of trees are mentioned in the Bible, including the olive, fig, cedar, almond, acacia, apple, oak, cypress, pomegranate, sycamore, terebinth, and willow. With so many references to trees and the products they yield, I think it's safe to say that God is a tree lover.

JERKY BREAK

The familiar culinary word *jerky* comes from the ancient Inca empire era and the word *ch'arki*, which means "to burn meat." Many modern hunters like me owe thanks to the guy or gal who discovered the jerky-making process, because there's nothing like a venison jerky break in a deer stand (especially when the jerky is teriyaki flavored). After a couple hours of intense watching and listening, the sudden thrill of remembering that the tasty meat treat is in my backpack helps spur me to greater feats of patience. And then, to quietly take a strip out and munch on it—now that's just joy on steroids.

ADMIT AND SUBMIT

A skein of geese flying in a V formation is always an amazing sight to behold—but it can also teach a valuable lesson in leadership. The job of being the lead bird and taking the brunt of the wind resistance requires maximum and constant effort, and the energy expenditure is not sustainable throughout the duration of a long flight. At some point before exhaustion takes its toll, the lead bird will, for the sake of the team, "admit and submit." He "admits" he's tired, pulls out, and submits to another bird's lead.

This leader-swapping tactic that contributes to a flock of geese staying airborne for unusually long stretches of time could also serve humans well. From governments to businesses, schools to churches, it's always good to get some fresh "wings" at the front of the formation. The only thing worse than a worn-out leader is one who actually recognizes that he's too tired for the job but still refuses to "admit and submit." Sooner or later he'll crash and burn, and the whole skein will suffer.

EVERY HUNTER SHOULD KNOW...

- If you have to choose between a new rifle and a new lawn mower, you have entirely too much yard.

- The key to making a 500-yard shot with a rifle is to move 300 yards closer.[18]

❧ Deer Tip ❧

If you're walking to your stand location and you see a pile of fresh deer droppings, I suggest that you step on them and squash them firmly, letting the odor of the pellets attach to the soles of your shoes. The residual smell is familiar to the keen nose of a deer and can help cover unnatural smells you may have collected on the bottoms of your boots before you came to the woods.

REMEMBER

Many hunters like to memorialize their experience of taking an animal with the awesome and amazing process of taxidermy. Around my house, you'll find wall mounts of the two biggest deer ever taken anywhere at any time. One is a simple honey-stained wooden plaque holding a gnarly set of five-points attached to just a small portion of a skull. The other is a more artistic mount of a two-year-old buck with a small basket rack of six points.

Neither of them come close to making the *Boone and Crockett* records book, but the reason I consider them to be the "biggest" bucks ever killed is because the five-point was my first deer and the six-point was my son's first. Both mounts are permanent reminders of some joyful moments we had in the great outdoors.

I also enjoy seeing my son's first squirrel—a big red brute that he took while I stood behind him. It weighed in just a few ounces shy of three pounds. Then there are two sets of antlers from our first six-by-six elks taken in the great state of Montana. There's a toothy, archery-killed javelina from Arizona sporting an aging Dale Earnhardt number-three baseball cap on its head, as well as a plaque-mounted display of a four-bearded turkey (which was taken by my friend Lindsey, who donated it to my wall because I sacrificed my chance to take the bird in deference to his chance to tag it). There's also a European skull mount of a very symmetrical Michigan eight pointer I took on camera for a popular outdoor TV show. Finally, but with great bravado, there's a massive rug hanging in my "cave" made from a huge

Alaskan brown bear that came in range of my rifle. Without exception, each time I look at it my mind fills with the incredible, expansive vistas of the "last frontier" and that rocky shoreline where the bear went down.

These few, very personal trophies are precious to me, and I cherish every memory connected to them—but I must admit I'm hopeful that they fulfill another purpose. When I'm dead and gone, perhaps someone will see those mounted, stuffed exploits and remember that I was here, that I lived and breathed, that I loved and was loved.

ARROWS AND ORNAMENTS

My wife, Annie, asking me a question in early September after seeing me bring home another dozen high-priced arrows: "Did you need those?"

Me: "Oh yes, babe. I need new sticks every year. It's a safety thing. I do it for you."

Me, asking Annie a question in early December while seeing her buy a collection of 12 Christmas ornaments: "What are you doing?"

Annie: "I'm buying arrows."

Me: Quietly and wisely heading to the truck.

NATHAN CHADMAN
CA FIRST DEER

SC

FOR BETTER SLEEP...

I have some good advice for hunters who want to avoid the sleep-stealing dilemma of a bothered conscience. Beware of someone grinning impishly as they suggest that as long as you don't check in every kill, you'll always have a tag in your possession if you're stopped by a game warden. Not cool. I realize that with the introduction of online game check-in, the temptation is even greater to cheat the system—but you'll get deeper and better rest if you obey the rules.

Turkey Tip

If you're cruising around a farm on foot and calling in an effort to locate a talkative gobbler, and you hear the excited screaming of a murder of crows, don't be annoyed. Instead, consider the good fortune that could come with that sound. Very often crows will angrily caw at the sight of a strutting bird—or two. Because they may be providing a clue to where the big boys are, it's worth your time to carefully head toward them and check out the scene. The only thing you'll lose if the crows are agitated by something other than strutting turkeys is a few calories—and that's never a bad thing.

⇥ Outdoor Poetry ⇤

He got up at four this morning
She heard him makin' coffee
He knows she thinks he's out of his mind
He was goin' to find a gobbler
Shoot him in the wattle
He was needin' somethin' tasty to fry
She said, "Honey, this is crazy"
He said, "It's just how Daddy raised me
No place I'd rather be at sunrise
I wanna hear 'em thunder
Till the day they put me under
I was born to outsmart those beady eyes!

"Baby, it's turkey time
Baby, it's turkey time
You know I need to do it
Gotta get back to it
Baby, it's turkey time"

Well, there he was in the woods
Hopin' he would do some good
She called him on his cell-phone wire
She said, "Babe, I need to tell ya
Your boss is callin' for ya
He said, 'You better get there quick, or you'll be fired' "

Then all at once he had a problem
He could hear 'em gobblin'
They were comin' down that old loggin' road
He said, "Babe, I got a situation
Right now my heart is racin'
Gotta sit down quick and let you go

'Cause baby, it's turkey time
Baby, it's turkey time
You know I need to do it
Gotta get back to it
Baby, it's turkey time"[19]

JUST WONDERING

If a tree falls in the forest and destroys that high-dollar lock-on stand you left hanging in it, and neither you nor anyone else is around to hear it, does it still make that "cha-ching" sound when it hits the ground?

DEER DANDER

An allergy to the dander of deer, elk, and other big game is not uncommon among hunters. I'm convinced that I deal with it, though my allergy is not as serious as others'. If the weather is on the warmer side when I field dress a deer, I sometimes sense a slight numbing of my lips, an indicator that my reaction is very slight but very real.

My son, on the other hand, has had a more serious reaction to dander after handling whitetail deer—to the point of bluing lips and dangerously shallow breathing. For that reason, it is a trait that cannot be ignored.

On the positive side, Nathan and I agree that we need to hunt big game more often and more places in order to eliminate more of the dander-yielding animals, all for the sake of our health and the well-being of our fellow hunters who are also prone to suffer from this unique condition.

WHEN STILLNESS FALLS

If a grown man chokes up and fights the urge to cry as he tells a story, it's an obvious sign to me that he feels something very deeply. Such was the case with a gentleman named Charlie Thomas, who drove me to the Norfolk, Virginia, airport for my return to Tennessee after I spoke at a sportsman's event in Suffolk.

We talked about our mutual enjoyment of hunting deer and

shared a few of our favorite experiences. At the top of his list of unforgettable moments in the deer stand was an account that didn't involve a battle of wits with an antlered beast. Instead, it was about something much more memorable.

Charlie told me that one afternoon he sat in the woods, which were filled with the usual, enjoyable sounds of chirping birds, scampering squirrels, and the gentle rustle of leaves swaying with a slight stirring breeze. He smiled as he recalled what hunters often refer to as the pleasurable mix of nature's "music." He paused in thought for a couple seconds as if to imply that something very personal and very moving for him was about to be revealed.

"All at once," he said, whisper-like, as if he was glad to be transported back to the scene and remember it again, "the woods went completely quiet. It was strange how the wind stopped dead and the critters hushed. Not a sound. It was tomb-like where I sat."

He paused again, longer this time. I looked over at him and could see that he was caught up in an emotion that had stolen his ability to talk.

As he stared straight ahead and drove, he struggled to continue his account of the experience. Describing a silence that he not only heard but seemed to feel, he said in a broken voice, "All at once a verse in Psalm 46 came to my mind. Verse 10 says, 'Be still, and know that I am God.'"[20] The words poured from him slowly, affectionately and almost musically.

He teared up but forced himself to go on. "I was completely overwhelmed with a sense that God Himself had given me a chance to literally live the words of the verse that was so fitting for the moment. I can't explain how stunned I was, how humbled I felt, and how deeply grateful I was for the gift of stillness that had fallen around me. I had never known that level of awareness of God's presence, and all I could do was raise my eyes to heaven and worship Him.

"The silence didn't last long, maybe less than a minute, but the memory of the moment lingers in my heart and will be there until I meet the One who gave it to me face-to-face."

When Charlie finished telling about his "be still and know" encounter, I was speechless as I processed how inspired I felt by his heartfelt and well-told experience. I determined then and there to never again ignore a sudden silence that can happen in a deer stand or any other outdoor setting, because it could very well be more than an ordinary occurrence. It could be divine.

LEAVE IT TO BEAVER

My Nebraskan friend and fellow weaver of words, D. Jake Roberts, writes a weekly column targeted to lovers of the outdoors called "Treestand Chatter." He kindly permitted me to include one of my favorites, which features some interesting thoughts and facts about an animal I have found to be unusually wary of my presence—an animal that has managed to test my ticker a time or two with its ear-bursting protest of my pre-dawn or post-sunset invasion of its world. The column article is titled "Leave It to Beaver."

In the intriguing world of animals, there stands a figure by ponds and rivers and large trees balanced firmly on its two rear webbed feet and anchored by its wide scaly and flat fatty-tissued tail. With gaudy orange iron-chiseled front teeth they can amazingly fell *very* large trees. Lacking magnesium, their pre"pond"erance of iron within their body supplies constantly growing front chisel-teeth (a bit ugly—except to one another, I suppose).

Next to humans they are said to be the second most skilled constructionists!

It takes us humanoids 20 years and more to produce engineers of this degree of skill. You don't have to walk very far along riverbanks before coming across signs of their work (or destruction in some eyes, especially when your favorite ancient mega tree lies dead in the water).

Jaymi Heimbuch has summarized "eight things to know about nature's most impressive landscape engineers."[21] She discusses the beaver's ability to thwart drought, help against pollution, and indeed the scope and long-lasting changes that a beaver family can bring to an ecosystem are incredible.

Two particular events have stirred my deepest beaver-awe: 1) Wading well above my waistline while fly-fishing after dark, flinging a number-six phony *hexagenia limbata* (*big* mayfly) over a large gulping *Salmo trutta* (brown trout)…an unsuspecting beaver and I were apparently sharing the same spot on the river. He warily discovered me first. With an enormous thrust of power his large flat rudder whopped the water's surface only four feet away. Water now dripped from my eyeglasses and, admittedly, also down the insides of my pant-legs. I instantly shock-shouted!

2) Two weeks ago I helped hoist a 50-pound chisel-tooth up the river's edge. I couldn't stop gawking.

The day before I had witnessed him bolting underwater with amazing speed and skill. Studying his webs this next day I could now understand its swimming prowess.

The very orange incisors…I then better understood the submissive demise of the trees once standing tall at bank-side. Drenched fur was completely dry and warm beneath its guard hairs, helping me understand quality of life beneath an icy river-flow.

I don't understand how, but now maybe why, such a creature even came to exist…perfectly designed and equipped for its environment and tasks! Really?

Their construction sites, huts, and food-storage banks (fresh twiglets preserved and stockpiled for wintertime luxury dining)…wow! As an educator I have marveled and observed learning curves of human two- to three-year-olds. Learning curves of adult two- to three-year-old beavers (some have lived as long as twenty-four years) can allow walking on hind feet while carrying a bundle of twigs tray-like in their arms. Learning curve? It's a young rodent. It's a "castoroide" secreting a vanilla-scented goo used for food flavoring.

God thought of, designed, constructed, and provided a means for beaver self-perpetuation. I think the word "awesome" is particularly appropriate here. A brain about the size of a golf ball…learning curve? Leave it to beaver! I'd like to take this moment to praise the Lord Jesus Christ…the Creator of the beaver.[22]

JAKE ROBERTS

MARK
1:17

A TIME TO REMEMBER...
AND LAUGH

Because hunting often includes long stretches of time waiting quietly for something to appear, I've found that it's a good opportunity to simply think about things. My thoughts can range from how to do a task waiting for me when I get home to what I'll say when I call a young friend who wants some marital advice. Or I might rehearse a keynote speech I'll be giving at a wild-game dinner event.

Sometimes—and I love this—my memory vault opens, and I walk in and enjoy reliving an experience from the past...which can cause a good, soul-healing laugh. Such is the case when I recalled what happened one summer morning in 1973.

After getting discharged from the US Navy, I purchased a high-mileage 1963 Chevrolet Biscayne; stopped getting haircuts; donned some bell-bottom blue jeans, a flannel shirt, and some shin-high leather cowboy boots; tossed my guitar in the passenger seat of my new car; and took off across country on a free-spirit, no-real-destination adventure across America.

I drove westward from West Virginia, heading first to the Dallas, Texas, area. My plan was to stop at my uncle Norman's house in the heart of the big city and mooch—er, stay the night with them—before striking out for the deserts of west Texas and Arizona. I drove all day and way into the night before finally arriving in the neighborhood where my uncle lived. I found the address and pulled into his driveway. It was nearly three o'clock in the morning and, wanting to show some good manners, I didn't knock on the door. After all, they didn't know I was coming, so they weren't expecting me. So I snuggled into the back seat of the Biscayne and fell into a sound sleep.

It didn't take long for the early-morning Texas sun to heat up the car and rouse me from my slumber. I looked at my watch. *Surely my kinfolk would be up at seven*, I thought. Looking forward to just the possibility of Aunt Mary's hot breakfast, I climbed out of the car, stretched like a cat in the driveway, walked up onto the porch of my relatives' house, and firmly knocked on the door.

What a surprise I had.

An unfamiliar fellow behind the storm door nervously asked, "Who are you, and why are you knocking on our door at this hour?"

I answered, "And who are you?" I got no answer. He simply returned a curious stare, so I continued, "Am I at the home of Norman Chapman?" I quoted the address I had been given.

The stunned resident kept his hand on the handle of the storm door and said, "Uh…yes and no."

He could see the puzzled look on my face, and I could see a little bit of relief on his as he explained, "Yes, you are at that address, but this is not the home of Norman Chapman."

"What?" I thought I was dreaming.

"Well," the fellow said with a smile, "the Chapmans finished moving out early yesterday morning, and we moved in last night. They're now living sixty miles north of here."

I apologized for giving him a scare and for sleeping in his driveway. I also told him how glad I was that he didn't get up in the middle of the night and call the cops on me.

The two of us laughed that morning in Texas—and as I remembered the moment while hunting, I had another good chuckle. They say laughter is good medicine. I say it's extra potent when it's had in a deer stand.

FIELDS OF TRUTH

On one of the farms I hunt there are several large fields that I walk across. Each one is a living illustration of some notable Bible verses.

For example, around late March or early April, when turkey season gets underway, the farmer turns the moist surface of a field with a plow and drops seed into the broken soil. Thus begins a process that's referred to in the book of John: "Truly, truly, I say to you, unless a grain of wheat falls into the earth and dies, it remains alone; but if it dies, it bears much fruit" (12:24).

A few months later, when the early archery portion of deer season arrives, a field with a ripened crop ready to harvest provides a picture of another verse in John: "Do you not say, 'There are yet four months, and then comes the harvest'? Behold, I say to you, lift up your eyes and look on the fields, that they are white for harvest" (4:35).

And a field of wildflowers speaks of God's provision: "Why are you anxious about clothing? Consider the lilies of the field, how they grow: they neither toil nor spin, yet I tell you, even Solomon in all his glory was not arrayed like one of these. But if God so clothes the grass of the field, which today is alive and tomorrow is thrown into the oven, will he not much more clothe you, O you of little faith?" (Matthew 6:28-30 ESV).

SINGING TREES

While walking through a huge stand of spruce trees during an elk hunt high on a Montana mountain, I stopped to rest for a few minutes. As I waited in hopes of hearing a bull bugle in the area, I realized the elk had to contend with some competition—the sound of the wind singing in the evergreens. It seemed that every needle in every tree around me responded like a choir member under the direction of the arms of the swaying branches.

I could've been annoyed by the sustained singing. Instead, I closed my eyes, enjoyed the song, and gladly did what this verse says to do:

> Let the trees of the forest sing,
> let them sing for joy before the LORD,
> for he comes to judge the earth (1 Chronicles 16:33 NIV).

BOBCAT SIGHTING

Consider it an uncommon treat when you spot a big bobcat while hunting. The males can be very solitary and have been known to range as many as 16 miles in warmer weather to 40 miles in the winter. Normally, if you see one it's a momentary encounter—that is, unless there's something about you that looks like a rabbit. If so, just hope you see the bobcat before it sees you.

INSULTED BY A SKUNK

I sat on the ground with my back against a red oak at the edge of a field, wishing for a springtime gobbler or two to show up. As I carefully watched the tree line for the appearance of a brilliant white head atop a deep red neck, I just happened to catch movement to my right.

Thinking it could be a bearded bird on the move, I slowly moved only my gaze as far as it would go toward the intruder and then began to rotate my head gradually in the direction of whatever creature was approaching.

My heart sank when I saw the distinct black and white fur of a skunk. It lumbered in my direction through the ankle-high grass at the edge of the field. As it got closer, I got nervous. With the intention of not being noisy and messing up my turkey hunt, I breathily said to the skunk, "Git! Git out of here!"

I didn't want to create a lot of motion and wave my arms to

scare away the skunk, but by then the little stinker was getting close enough for me to consider breaking that rule. I realized that if I didn't quickly take more drastic measures, the menace could get close enough to give me a face full of its "perfume" if I scared it.

Not wanting to go through the cleansing process required to return to social acceptance after a skunk dousing, I decided to eliminate the possibility with my 12-gauge pump. When the skunk came within 15 yards of where I sat, I put my forefinger on the safety button.

Just before I raised my gun, he (or she—I couldn't tell) suddenly stopped in its tracks, raised its head, and sniffed the air. Three or four seconds later it wheeled around on its hind paws and took off running.

I felt grateful that I didn't have to expend a perfectly good shotgun shell on an inedible critter. My turkey hunt was salvaged. I relaxed my grip on the gun and smiled—until the disturbing, self-esteem-crushing thought occurred to me, *I was just winded by a skunk.*

Nature is schoolmistress, the soul the pupil; and whatever one has taught or the other has learned has come from God—the Teacher of the teacher.

Tertullian

BASS TALK

A dad fishing with his son, who got in big trouble at school for sassing his teacher, said, "If that big bass you just caught that's in the live well could talk to you about what happened at school, do you know what he'd say to you, Son?

Son: "No, sir. What would he say?"

Dad: "Sometimes it's better to keep your mouth shut."

Deer Tip

There's no need to look at your field of overgrown, waist-high grass as an area to avoid. Instead, see the field as an opportunity to direct deer to where you are. This tactic works best if the following steps are taken about six weeks before the fall hunting season begins.

- Do some scouting along the edges of the field and determine the location of trails leading into the field. Likely you'll see pressed-grass evidence of often-used paths that the deer seem to favor. Keep in mind that there could be several entry points up and down the field.

- Using a string trimmer or mowing machine that can cut a path about three feet wide, create a trail through the thick grass that is obvious to the eyes. Continue the cut across the field to an exit point that goes under a tree where you can hang a lock-on deer stand or place a leaning ladder stand. Because deer tend to take the line of least resistance when it comes to crossing an overgrown field, the likelihood of them coming under your position is very good.

Don't forget, deer will use the trail going both ways, so be sure to place your stand so you can monitor both the field and the woods. When this method works for you, you're welcome to thank me with some fresh backstrap.

Turkey Tip

A gobbler's eyes are his best defense against your intention to take him home to your skillet. Turkey peepers are highly skilled at spotting the least amount of movement, and a spooked bird will not hesitate to escape any perceived danger.

For that reason, if you're caught off guard and not in position to take a shot when a bearded bird approaches, your best hope is that he's in the mood to show his stuff by raising his fan. If he does go into a full strut, this will be the best chance you'll have to get your gun up.

Be patient and remember that a tom will typically spin as he struts. When you see the back side of his widespread fan, that's when he can't see you. If that happens, you have two or three seconds to quietly raise your turkey taker and close the deal.

SC

THE LOCAL BRAIN-WASH

Our son tagged a really nice eight-point buck, and his wife requested a European style mount of the head for a decor idea she had. I had never attempted any type of taxidermy but welcomed the adventure. Plus, I figured I could save some cash by doing it myself. So I did what most of us do these days when we want to learn something we've never tried before—I went to YouTube.

Following the instructions on a video I found, I used a knife to remove the hide and as much meat as possible from the skull, then I boiled the skull in salty water for two hours. The online instructor noted that removing the brains would be a tricky task and suggested using a spoon, but the rest of the meat could be removed with a power washer.

I didn't own a power washer, but I got excited when the ingenious idea came to go to the local car wash and use their pressurized sprayer. On the way I realized I forgot to spoon out the brains before I left. Not wanting to backtrack, I decided to see if I could do it at the car wash instead.

For only five dollars I had fifteen minutes to de-meat and de-brain the skull. The power sprayer worked fabulously—except for one thing. When I poked the nozzle into the inch-and-a-half-wide opening of the brain section, which was lodged between my feet facing upward, I didn't realize what was about to happen. The instant I pulled the trigger, the jet stream had nowhere to go but upward. Mushy, grayish matter shot out of the rounded cavity directly at my face.

The disgusting clumps of mind-matter stuck to the skin on my forehead and cheeks like goop. Fortunately, I was wearing my glasses. I spent the last five of my fifteen paid minutes of car-wash time wiping deer brains off my face, fighting an embarrassing gag reflex, and mumbling about the disgusting fact that I had just brain-washed myself.

DUCK!

If your name is Will, you might reconsider accepting an invitation to go duck hunting with a large party. In the excitement of the moment, when a huge flock of ducks is coming in, someone could yell, "Fire at will!" If so, the only suggestion I have is… duck!

AN INFAMOUS PROVERB

The great philosopher Zebco Shakespeare said, "Give a man a fish and he'll eat for a day. Teach a man to fish and he'll buy a bunch of rods and reels, a bucket full of bait, a big boat, and a truck with which to pull it—and he'll head to the lake where he'll sit in the boat all day to catch a fish to give to his family who will eat for a day."

HELP FOR HUSBANDS

If you are a husband who loves to hunt deer, you should keep this important marriage-saving advice in mind. If you leave your house to go to the woods, and you hear your wife say, "Have fun," that's a good sign. And when you get home, and she appears genuinely interested as she asks, "See anything?" then you can rest in knowing that you're doing something right as a husband.

If, on the other hand, as you leave the house she says, "I hope your gun jams," and when you return she asks, "Are you home already?"—then you'll know you have work to do on your relationships with both your dear and your deer.

TAKE YOUR TIME, MR. TAXIDERMIST

Have you ever wondered why it's really good that it takes months for a taxidermist to process your trophy and get it back to you? I can tell you from experience why the wait is a blessing. It's because after you announce to your wife that there'll be another dead animal taking up yet another wall in "her" house, and you tell her what it's going to cost to put it there, she's going to need a long time to get over it—assuming she does. So, take your time, Mr. Taxidermist!

WHERE GREATNESS IS FOUND

When I prepared to take a shot at a 300-pound black bear during a springtime hunt in Montana, my friend Eddy was behind me, filming the process. What happened became a cause for some embarrassment. The edited footage reveals the story because I added titles at the bottom of the screen as the shot played out.

- "Ready." I rest my rifle on a tree and put the crosshairs on the bear's vitals.

- "Aim." Several seconds pass as I wait for the bear to position himself for a high-percentage kill shot.

- "Load!" Yep. That dreaded word comes up in the caption area of the footage after I pull the trigger. What you can hear in the audio is not the loud report of my .270 caliber rifle. Instead, it is the distinct metallic click that announces, "Duh! Chapman didn't chamber a cartridge."

My reaction on film to the blunder was a motionless and speechless pause of about five seconds. There were two good reasons for that pause. One, I didn't want to turn around and look at the gallery of two (Eddy and the guide) behind me and face the music that didn't play from my .270. Two, I decided it was better to watch the bear in the scope to determine if he'd heard the slamming of the firing pin that to me sounded like the crack of a fired .22 rifle. Apparently the bear hadn't heard anything unusual, and Eddy kept the camera rolling.

Though stunned by my no-bullet blunder, I kept an eye on the bear while I carefully moved my right hand to the bolt and chambered a round slowly and quietly in order not to alert the bear. My target remained where it had been when his life had been spared moments earlier, but his fate was about to change.

One shot did the deed. I later added the following words to the edited footage, which I had heard a year or two earlier (when I had managed to do something right, but only after first trying and bitterly failing): "Greatness is not found in perfection—it's found in recovery." Maybe you'll remember those words the next time you get ready, aim, and load.

PREACH IT!

Hunter to his pastor: "Preacher, do you think it's a sin for me to hunt on Sunday?"

Pastor: "From what I've heard about the way you shoot, it's a sin for you to hunt any day of the week."[23]

UNEXPECTED SOUNDS

There are three unexpected sounds I've heard more than once in the woods that I'm convinced have done more to remove the dark brown pigment from my hair than just about anything else I've experienced in life. They are…

- the ear-piercing snort of a startled deer that I didn't know was near me, especially in the dark when I'm walking to my stand before daylight or leaving it after sunset.

- a tight-sitting grouse that feels like I'm much too close for its comfort but waits until my boot is right beside it to blast out of its resting place.

- the ghoulish, chilling sound of a screech-owl that chooses to scream from its perch in a tree under which I just happen to be walking.

If you have white hair, then maybe you've been in those same woods.

NICE TRY

A hunter bragged shamelessly to his buddies about the deer he had taken that morning, which was lying in the bed of his pickup. "This thing is a beast, the biggest I've seen so far this season. There's enough meat on him to feed two families for a whole year." About that time, a game warden drove up. After asking for everyone's licenses and finding that the braggart didn't have one, he cited the guy $500 for not having a tag. The upset hunter protested. "Say what? You're gonna fine me for this scrawny little thing?"[24]

❧ Deer Tip ❧

If you're hunting over or near a fresh scrape, and a buck approaches that is typical in size but is either submissive in its posture (which can be hard to detect) or turning to look back (which is easy to notice), you should consider being patient and hold off on taking a shot. Why? Because a larger, more dominant buck could very well be close behind and the cause of the smaller buck's apparent humble demeanor.

APPLES OF GOLD

There's a proverb that says, "Like apples of gold in settings of silver is a word spoken in right circumstances" (Proverbs 25:11). I'm familiar with how sweet those golden apples can be. One of the times they were served to me on the silver platter of kindness was the day I came back to the cabin where I was lodging during a hunt with a doe.

The doe had looked a lot bigger in the peep sight mounted on my compound bowstring as I had taken aim at her. When I recovered the deer, I was stunned to discover it wasn't much bigger than a full-grown collie dog. Never willing to waste a deer, I basically threw it over my shoulder and headed back to the cabin.

Standing up on the deck was my friend and fellow deer hunter Don. He saw me coming up the hill toting my trophy-ette, and when he decided I was close enough to hear him he looked down and said with a smile, "Chapman, you are an incredible archer."

I felt supported with his comment—and then he added, "Anybody who can hit something that small is simply amazing." The words were indeed fitly spoken, yet they did just what my friend meant for them to do. They made me feel better.

MOVING A MOOSE

When I pulled into a McDonald's parking lot in a far-north town to grab a cup of coffee and saw a bull moose lying lifeless on a flatbed trailer, I was stunned at the incredible size of the animal. A crowd had gathered around it, and I was among the onlookers. Until that day I had never seen a real live moose— er, should I say "dead"?

As I gawked at the huge mound of soon-to-be freezer filler, the two hunters who were responsible for the trophy in transport came walking up. They looked completely worn out (though the gallery of the curious and all their questions about the bull seemed to energize them). When I realized what their haggard appearance implied, I was struck by the following thought.

The greatest challenge in hunting moose is not in coming up with the funds for a hunting trip, or finding a moose after arriving, or calling one in, or shooting such a massive beast. The real challenge is getting it home!

SOCIAL DISTANCING

The 2020 outbreak of COVID-19 resulted in a national attempt to minimize the spread of the deadly bug through a method that became known as "social distancing." The tactic of keeping our distance from others for a season in order to avoid contracting the virus and passing it on was a huge challenge for most citizens, but we hunters had no problem understanding and appreciating the idea for a simple reason: It's what we already do when we go to the woods. We do it intentionally and for as long and as often as we possibly can.

TERMS OF EN-"DEER"-MENT

- *In-"stand"-ity*: a word used for the mental defect that compels a hunter to get in a stand, think of another location that might be better, dismount and move, and then do it again another time or two during a single hunt.

- *"Doe"-cumentary*: a TV show that features a story about why and how hunters can and should do their part in controlling the deer population by taking and tagging at least one doe per season.

- *"Trigger"-nometry*: what a dad teaches his kid about the science of applying pressure slowly to a rifle trigger for the purpose of gaining the maximum accuracy.

- *"Art"-chery*: a dual-subject class created by a grandfather for his homeschooled grandkids using watercolors, brushes, bows, and arrows.

- *"Moose"-tery*: what a moose hunter calls the sudden, silent, unexplainable, and perplexing disappearance of a trophy bull that was there just a moment ago.

- *"Bullet"-zer Prize*: an award that could be given to every older hunter who passes on the heritage of hunting to the younger ones by taking the time and effort to write down their favorite outdoor adventures in a journal.

- *"Deer" John*: the opening salutation of a break-up note received by the boyfriend of the girl who would rather go hunting all day Saturday than hang out at the mall.

- *"Annie"-versary*: the one day of the year that all hunters who married a gal named Annie make the wise choice not to go to the woods to hunt. Instead, the husband devotes that day to celebrating and spending time with her. To do otherwise could result in him being sent to the dreaded "dark woods" of marital trouble. (I love you, Annie!)

TWO UNFORGETTABLES

In all my years of hunting whitetail bucks, two deer were especially memorable—and not because they hang on my wall. In fact, I didn't get a shot at either of them. One buck had a name; one had a number.

First there was "Aaron." I met him in New York State on a farm owned by the late and legendary whitetail expert Charles J. Alsheimer. During a visit with Charles, he invited me to climb aboard his Gator and go with him to check on the deer contained in his fenced acreage. The animals were fully wild but confined to an area where Charles studied their behavior and growth patterns and photographed them for a nearby university.

As he drove into a meadow at the foot of a densely wooded hillside, there were no deer to be found. He stopped the Gator, turned off the motor, and went to the tailgate. After filling a plastic jug two-thirds full with a mix of corn and oats, he stepped out into the meadow a few yards and said, "Come stand by me, watch, and listen." Then he proceeded to shake the jug. The grain inside made a distinct rattling sound. After about 15 seconds of shaking the jug, he stopped and said, "The deer on this property have learned what that sound means. They know it well and they know me. You're a stranger, but just stay close. You'll be fine."

I tuned my ears to the hillside, and about 45 seconds later I began to hear a faint but familiar sound. It was deer hooves crunching the dry leaves inside the edge of the woods. Slowly, one by one, three sizable female whitetails walked into the meadow. At Charles' request, I remained motionless and didn't say a word.

He poured the contents of the jug on the ground, and the furred trio approached. They were very cautious but seemed willing to risk our presence for the sake of a tasty snack.

Charles whispered, "Keep watching the edge of the woods to my left." A minute or so later my jaw dropped at the sight of the beast that exited the woods and walked toward us. It was a wide and tall 12-point buck with a spread of antlers well beyond his ears. I wondered how close he would come.

I was stunned when the heavy animal came within three feet of us and began to have his share of the grain on the ground. I had never been that close to what deer hunters refer to as a "monster buck," and those I had gotten close to were nowhere near as endowed antler-wise—plus, they were expired. This massive buck was so near me that I had to turn my head side to side to see the outer reaches of his main frame.

"Let me introduce you to Aaron. He's a four-year-old and named after my son." I was speechless as Charles continued. "Aaron is totally wild, and you wouldn't want to be in here with him during rut. He's the boss, and he'd let you know it. I've known him since he was a fawn, and he's been the subject of several studies I've done on whitetails, such as annual antler growth and how moon phases affect deer behavior."

As he told me more about the resident boss, Charles reached into his coat pocket and took out an apple and a knife. With the knife he sliced the apple into four quarters and then said, "Put your hand out flat." He then placed one of the apple quarters in my palm and said, "Now slowly reach out your hand toward Aaron."

With my hand out as instructed, I watched the big buck slowly move closer to us. I won't forget the feeling of awe that accompanied the presence of such an enormous, fully alive, and moving set of antlers. What happened next is forever etched in my memory.

The mighty buck looked at me, then looked at the apple piece and proceeded to eat the treat right out of my hand. I felt his cold nose on my skin when he took it. He raised his head and looked at us while he chomped on the fruit. As he did, Charles put the second of four pieces in my hand, and the beast took it. Within a couple minutes, the entire apple was gone and snack time was over for Aaron, except for partaking in what was left of the grain that the does had not eaten.

As we left the meadow, I thanked Charles for letting me share in his connection to such a majestic creature. While Aaron probably forgot about me before he made it back to the woods, the same is not true for me. I will always remember the day when I was privileged to have greatness eating out of my hand.

The second unforgettable deer I encountered was referred to simply as "Number Six." I met him near Wills Point, Texas, when I was in the area to keynote at a wild game dinner event. While there I was privileged to stay at the Malouf Ranch. I arrived on Thursday evening with plans to hunt on the property for wild hogs on Friday morning. As Tom Malouf showed me around the ranch, he asked if I'd be interested in accompanying him after the hunt the next morning to help him tranquilize one of his prize bucks and treat its injured hoof. Having never had that experience, I jumped at the chance.

Following the taking of my very first hog on Friday morning,

I joined Tom and his coworker Alan as they set out to locate Number Six. When the buck was spotted, I noted that he was antlerless. Though curious as to why his rack was missing while other bucks around him were still antlered, I didn't interrupt the process with an inquiry.

When the buck was located, we moved in close enough for Tom to deliver a dose of the tranquilizer to the deer's hip using a dart gun. Within 15 minutes the buck was snoozing soundly. As I filmed the process, Tom and Alan covered the deer's face with a cloth and loaded the sleeping buck onto a gurney, then headed back to the building where the doctoring would take place.

With a window of around 45 minutes within which to work before the injured buck would rouse from the effects of the tranquilizer, Tom worked quickly. While he cleaned the injured hoof, he directed me in the gauze-cutting and wound-wrapping duties. I felt rather surgeon-like as I helped. On occasion, when I wasn't cutting tape and dressing Number Six's hoof, I would stroke his neck. It was strange to feel the fur of a very alive deer under my hand.

When the treatment was finished, the buck was taken back to where he had fallen asleep. The three of us stood by at a distance and watched to make sure he woke up and was able to stand. Slowly the freshly doctored deer awoke and staggered to his hooves. After he gathered his footing, he wandered off daze-like but in good health.

It was a memorable thing to be hands-on with a deer that is considered a prime trophy, much less be able to help him run and walk again without a limp. At that point, however, I was not

totally sure why he was considered important enough to get the kind of medical attention he had received. That changed when I got back to the ranch facility with Tom and he opened a folder to show me what kind of deer I had just been close enough to that I could hold its hoof in my hand. It was an eye-popping photo of a nontypical buck sporting upward of 25 points in all directions, each extending several inches. I could hardly believe what I saw.

I learned that Number Six was a two-year-old breeder with a purpose of passing on his impressive antler-making genes to the young bucks that the local doe would deliver for him. It's no wonder he was a prize. I also discovered that his massive antler growth was improved by the protein-enhanced feed he consumed. (I was inspired to start eating more protein!) I wasn't surprised to learn that the mind-boggling rack he was carrying in the photo was removed a month or so earlier to relieve him of the heavy, neck-straining weight until the next summer arrived—when once again he would sprout a set of bones that would haunt the dreams of everyone who saw him. Just like he still does mine.

ENDURING THE JOURNEY

When I climbed into my friend's pickup truck that was fully loaded with our elk-hunting gear to begin the journey from Tennessee to Colorado for the 2018 season, the excitement needle was pegging to the far right. Our high energy at the time of our pre-dawn departure drove us to talk well into the afternoon about what we were heading out west to do.

Of course, the miles behind us and the slowly decreasing numbers on the GPS screen showing how many miles were left to go eventually began to take their toll on our bodies and tongues. Though we started to feel physically drained, our spirits couldn't be wearied by how many states we had yet to cross. Somewhere inside us was a reservoir of enthusiasm that motivated us to press on.

What was replenishing that reserve? Only another hunter could understand that our willingness to forge ahead was found in knowing what incredible sights and sounds—and hopefully some elk-hunting success—awaited us in the majestic territory of the Rockies.

That trip to Colorado is in the past now, but recalling how the thought of *getting* there constantly restored our joy while we were in the grueling throes of *going* there is similar to the way we feel as people of faith who are heading to an awesome place called heaven. The anticipation of someday arriving at the "city of God" helps us endure the long and often exhausting miles on the road of time. Here's a song about that destination—what reaching it means to us and why it keeps us pressing onward.

We Have a City

Some people wonder
How can we smile
As we journey through these dark and troubled days?
But there's a reason for our joy
While we walk these weary miles
We are headed to a far and better place

We have a city we are going to
Where our burdens will be gone; we believe it's true
With eyes of faith we see the gates that someday we'll walk through
We have a city we are going to

And we have loved ones
We'll see again
Who are waiting just beyond our final step
But best of all we'll meet our Savior there
Who washed away our sins
He's the hope that keeps us looking up ahead

Walls of jasper, streets of gold
Forever young, never old
Crystal waters, gates of pearl
Nothing like it in this world
No sorrow there, no one at war
Only peace forevermore
With angels we will sing along
When we arrive at our new home

We have a city we are going to
Where our burdens will be gone; we believe it's true
With eyes of faith we see the gates that someday we'll walk through
We have a city we are going to[25]

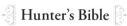

Hunter's Bible

*By faith he [Abraham] made his home in the promised
land like a stranger in a foreign country; he lived in
tents, as did Isaac and Jacob, who were heirs with
him of the same promise. For he was looking forward
to the city with foundations, whose architect and
builder is God…Here we do not have an enduring
city, but we are looking for the city that is to come.*

HEBREWS 11:9-10; 13:14 NIV

HUNTER OR KILLER?

A message came to my inbox from a fellow who read my first
book written for hunters (*A Look at Life from a Deer Stand*).
He asked me to expand on a statement I included in one of the
chapters that was made to my son when he was young and beginning to hunt deer with me. My point was that if my son had no
remorse after killing a deer, then he was a killer and not a hunter.
The following is my response to the sender's request.

> Thanks for reading my book, and I appreciate your
> request to elaborate on my comment about remorse
> after a kill. I tried to help my son understand that
> life is life, whether human or animal, and while we
> as humans have a God-given role as rulers over the

animals on the earth, it's important to respect the life that God gave them. Taking that life for a food source is not an evil act, but it is a serious one that, in my estimation, should not be done without at least some level of respectful awareness and appreciation for the animal's suffering and sacrifice. I hoped my son would embrace the attitude that killing an animal without an abiding respect for its life could influence how he feels about all forms of life…including and especially, human life.

I realize that the use of the word *killer* in reference to a hunter who kills an animal without feeling respect for its suffering is a strong assessment and could sound condemning, but again, my goal was and remains to help hunters—especially the young ones—avoid having a cavalier attitude about life in the woods and out of the woods.

It concerns me deeply that many youngsters today are inundated with opportunities to fall into an unfeeling outlook on the value of life through graphically violent video games that remove them from the reality of the pain that accompanies the taking of life. Hunting with a kid could actually help them recover and cultivate a needed respect (or "remorse," as I put it) for life as they shoot and fatally wound an animal and see the flow of real blood and watch as life drains from its body. That's the reality I wanted my son to embrace and remember when he wasn't hunting.

MORE MARRIAGE
ADVICE FOR HUNTERS

For my fellow hunters who wear a wedding ring, and for the guys who will someday put one on, here are five surefire ways to help your wife not hate what you love to do.

1. Let her know that safety is your number-one priority when it comes to the potential hazards of being a hunter. Among other things, this includes how, where, and when you handle firearms; your usage of tree stands; staying connected to her via cell phone while you're outdoors; being weather-wise; and never risking your life by buying a new four-wheel-drive truck without her knowledge and approval.

2. Make every effort to honor her wishes when it comes to being present for important family events such as holiday dinners, weddings, funerals, graduations, and especially the birth of your children.

3. It's highly recommended that you "earn" your hunting time by doing something nice for your wife. For example, is there a room she wants painted? If so, then lovingly volunteer to stop by the hardware store on your way home from work to pick up the paint, brushes, and drop cloths she'll need for starting the job while you're duck hunting with your buddies.

4. Never enter your residence after a hunt wearing mess-making, mud-caked boots or carrying a blood-dripping game bag or reeking of the pungent odor of Tink's Number 69, which can permanently alter the smell of wallpaper.

5. Be considerate of her desires when it comes to hanging taxidermy on the walls of her "nest." If she suggests that your six-by-six Montana elk be placed over the living room fireplace mantel for all to see, smile and graciously obey her wishes. If, however, she prefers that it be hung in the garage, then appeal to her by saying what a shame it would be not to openly display such a valuable work of art. And when she asks what that value is, then quietly head to the garage and clear a place for your bull.

FIVE WAYS TO GET YOUR
YOUNGSTERS OUTDOORS

1. Take your kids to an elevated shooting house big enough for two or more. Being in an enclosed space allows children to move around without spooking the biggest buck you'll ever see—because it will definitely show up if there's a restless kid with you.

2. Promise them a monetary reward if they'll go to the lake and fish with you. (Just don't tell them it'll be in the form of payments to the orthodontist for their braces, the optometrist for the third replacement of their lost or broken glasses, and the school for that shark outfit they'll wear on drama night).

3. Pique their interest in going outdoors with you by sharing stories about your own experiences with your dad in the wild. Be careful to tell about only the fun trips and avoid the not-so-enticing tales. For example, our son might want to keep it to himself that he went camping with his dad and came home with 47 seed ticks on his body, and his dad had to use a paint scraper to remove the pesky little bloodsuckers.

4. Purchase a child-sized bow and arrow set, teach them how to use it, and never, ever turn your back on them when you're downrange pulling arrows out of the homemade hay-bale target in your backyard.

5. Take them to the hunter's safety course, where they'll be with other boys and girls their age who are also learning how and why to respect firearms. To drive home the importance of safely handling a weapon of any type, you can tell them what a gun-shop owner told me when I purchased my first pistol and asked him to give me his best advice regarding the handling of my new 9mm Smith and Wesson. With an obvious, sincere concern for his inexperienced customer and as much humility as he could muster, he respectfully said, "If Jesus hands the gun to you and tells you it's not loaded, check it anyway. He'll call you wise."

GET TO THE POINT

Me: Dialing my wife's cell-phone number about ten minutes after sunrise as my hands shake nearly uncontrollably following a crossbow shot at the biggest buck I had ever taken.

Annie: Answering the call with an obviously drowsy, pillow-muffled, "Hello?"

Me: Through breathing still heavy from the adrenaline rush that came with the monster-buck encounter, "Hey babe, I just shot a sixteen."

Annie: After a long pause, "Would that be points or pounds?"

COW STARES

Have you ever walked through a herd of cows in order to get to a deer stand or turkey blind? If so, have you noticed how they continue to chew the cud as they just stand and stare at you? I don't know about you, but I find their deadpan stare to be downright spooky. I don't trust staring cows. They make me feel like they're deciding between not letting my presence disturb their snack or attacking me. I'm tempted to take off running when the worry gets overly intense—but I fight the urge, move on, and watch my back.

⤜ Outdoor Poetry ⥤

When I see the sunrise, I think of you
How you're faithful and true to me
When I hear the bluebird's morning refrain
I hear your name so lovely

Sunny skies, your eyes
Sweet smell of the pine brings you to my mind
And when I walk these fields where the bonnets are blue
It's a lovely view…and I think of you

When I see the ivy that grows on the vine
I think of the time you grew on me
When I see the young fawns in the meadow at play
I think of the way I am with you

Sunny skies, your eyes
A warm April wind
Your touch on my skin
And when I walk these fields where the bonnets are blue
It's a lovely view…and I think of you

Sunny skies, your eyes
The dance of the stars
Your love in my heart
And when I walk these fields where the bonnets are blue
It's a lovely view…and I think of you[26]

CAMO-COVERED GIRL

When it comes to most hunters and reading, the only thing that could make them want to dive into a romance tale is if there is camo involved. So here ya go!

Rob and Marcy met their first year of college. He was from a midsize city in the south, and she came from a rural area in the northern part of the nation. Being raised in quite diverse settings and having so little in common in terms of their home locations, the likelihood of the two of them finding an interest in each other was slim. But that was before Cupid fired his love arrow at Rob's heart.

Upon entering the college cafeteria on his second day on campus, Rob caught a glimpse of his favorite camo pattern. Though he was a "city slicker," he was also an avid hunter and had been passionate about hunting since the first time he ventured to the woods as a ten-year-old with his dad.

Rob didn't see who was wearing the camo coat at first, but after a couple seconds his field of view widened, and he was surprised to see that the coat was sported by an athletic-looking female. He noticed how seemingly unconcerned the camo-covered girl was about being seen in such an untrendy fashion. As he headed to the serving line and watched out of the corner of his eye, the girl weaved her way around the tables toward him.

When she took her place in the line behind him, he turned to glance at her. In that brief moment he glimpsed a face framed by long blonde curls, and her deep blue eyes looked into his. That's when he heard angels sing in his head.

Flustered by the girl's nearness, Rob was unable to speak—though he wanted to. As he nervously fumbled with a tray and handful of silverware, he quickly thought about what he could say. The only thing that felt right was to make a reference to her jacket, along with how and why he was familiar with its style. He drew a deep breath, looked over his shoulder at her, and took a chance.

"Hi! I'm Rob, I like your coat, I have one with the same camo pattern, I wear it when I hunt, would that be something you like to do too?"

Knowing he had just delivered a grammar-rule-breaking run-on sentence, Rob braced himself for some rolling eyes and a firm rejection. He couldn't believe his ears when he heard, "It is!"

With that response, Rob heard violins join in with the singing angels. He knew what to say next.

"Deer? Turkey?"

The girl shrugged her shoulders in a friendly way and answered, "Both—and pheasants too. Lots of 'em where I'm from, and you gotta have a dog in the hunt. Love the dogs. And you?"

Rob had to force himself not to sound breathless as he said, "Definitely deer. Whitetail mostly, but I've been out west for mulies. And gobblers—now there's a smart bird. Besides how they taste, the fact that they're hard to outsmart is the main reason I like to hunt 'em. But I haven't had the chance to hunt pheasants." He stepped forward as the line moved and asked, "What's your name?"

"Marcy."

Rob couldn't resist teasing her. "Oh, Marcy me, that's a pretty name."

She smiled again and said, "Thanks. That's what my dad calls me. How'd you know that?"

Rob did a mental fist pump to celebrate that his attempt at a little levity didn't offend the huntress and, instead, made her smile.

When Marcy accepted his invitation to sit together in the cafeteria and share more about their mutual interest in hunting, Rob could hear an entire heavenly symphony in his head. For him, it was love at first "open sights."

An hour later, in mid-discussion of the pros and cons of baiting deer, Marcy looked at her phone to check the time and abruptly stood to her feet. "Oh wow!

I have five minutes to get to class, and it's a seven-minute walk across campus. I gotta go. Let's continue tomorrow at breakfast. Want to?"

Answering with a firm, "I'd love to," Rob stood up and put his hand out to shake on it. When Marcy's hand slipped into his and she gripped it tight, Rob determined then and there what trail he wanted to walk through the woods of his life. His new friend walked out of the cafeteria through the glass doors, and he watched her hurry down the sidewalk as he whispered an eyes-open prayer.

"God in heaven, You're the Maker of earth and all the beautiful and lovely things in it, and I have to say that You did especially good with Marcy. Thank You for letting our trails cross today, and please help me not mess up this opportunity."

Rob said, "Amen," and took a sip of his soda. He had no idea that Marcy had prayed, too, as she trotted to her class. "Dear God, how in the world am I going to tell my dad and mom that I met the man of my dreams on the second day of college?"

Reading about nature is fine, but if a person walks in the woods and listens carefully, he can learn more than what is in books, for they speak with the voice of God.

GEORGE WASHINGTON CARVER

❧ Hunter's Hint ❧

The upper and lower portions of a compound bow are not just useful for launching your arrows. Consider these ideas…

- Attach a two-to-three-inch string off the limb to use for determining wind direction. The thinner the string, the better its response will be to the wind, especially if it's slight.

- A small digital watch (minus the band) mounted to the inside of the lower limb close to the grip with two-sided tape will free you from making deer-alerting motion when you need to check the time.

- If you have lighted sights, it's a good idea to carry extra, easily accessible batteries. Assuming that multiple button-type batteries are required, wrap an extra set in paper or plastic, press them onto the sticky side of a two-inch square of good quality duct tape, and mount the square on the inside of your upper limb near the top of the riser.

- For the sake of identification in the event of an accident that would leave you unable to communicate, write your name, address, and phone number either on the riser with a permanent marker or on a piece of paper that can be adhered with clear tape to the inside of one of the limbs.

The information should be typed or clearly handwritten.

- If you'd like to memorize more Scripture passages, the inside of the limbs is also a great place to temporarily tape verses where you can easily see them.

YOU DECIDE

Regarding the introduction of the video camera to hunting, I've been asked if it's good or not so good. My answer is that I have mixed feelings about it, because filming a hunt with a smartphone or video camera has both benefits and drawbacks. I've dealt with both. For that reason, I usually offer the inquirer the following observations and say, "You decide."

Benefits

- A video can document a memory not only for the hunter, but also for family and friends.

- Playback can yield important and useful details about the shot, including the hunter's execution, the effectiveness of the arrow or bullet placement, and the direction the wounded animal ran after the shot.

- A hunting video can be an instructional tool to help younger hunters better prepare for their pursuits.

- Good quality hunting videos packaged and sold or posted online can become revenue-yielding products as well as a tutorial resource for those seeking to improve their hunting skills.

Drawbacks

- When self-filming, fumbling with a camera can not only cause a hunter to miss seeing an approaching animal, but it can also potentially hinder the concentration necessary for making a quick and merciful shot.

- The presence of video equipment can too easily swing the focus away from the hunted and put it on the hunter. If this imbalance happens, the hunt can become ego driven and lessen the quality of the experience.

- Killing an animal while hunting is an innately intense act that always results in blood flow. Most hunters accept that reality. But if the images of the kill are shown with an unedited, gratuitous, over-the-top display of blood, respect for hunting could be lost by those who see the video.

PARTING WORDS

I thought I had the best line about the brevity of life when I said to my doctor during an annual exam, "If you live long enough, it'll kill you." He gave a courtesy chuckle and said, "I have one better than that." I didn't believe him until he said, "Good health is the slowest form of death." I lost the contest but appreciated the good dose of medicinal laughter.

The doctor's statement is humorous indeed, but the truth is, those words have two barrels aiming at me and all my fellow hunters. One barrel blasts the truth that we need to take care of ourselves for the sake of increasing our longevity, while the other barrel delivers the sobering load of reality that everyone has an expiration date. My personal goal is to do the best I can to hang around as long as possible by eating wisely, getting frequent exercise, and casting my worries on the Lord, who cares for me.

That said, even with my best efforts to prolong the inevitable, I'm aware that eventually I will hear the call heard by the dad in the following song. Until I do, I want to enjoy every chance I have to head to the woods—where I can take a seat, savor the view, rest deeply, and occasionally whisper, "The buck stops here." I hope the same for you.

The Hunt Is Over

Daddy's old truck, smell of coffee in his cup
And how the highway seemed so empty at four a.m.
These are things I remember as we headed to the timber
We were off to chase the whitetails again

Cold November stand, golden sunrise on the land
And how the big ones could appear just like a ghost
The sun going down, that's when I'd hear the sound
Of Daddy's words he knew I dreaded most...

"It's time to go, the hunt is over
Throw that old Winchester gun across your shoulder
I know it's been good, son, to be here in these woods
But it's time to go on home
The hunt is over"

When I got my first deer, I thought I saw a tear
Running down that smile on Daddy's face
He said, "You might pull the trigger someday on something bigger
But son, this is one you can't replace

"And now it's time to go, the hunt is over
Throw that old Winchester gun across your shoulder
I know it's been good, son, to be here in these woods
But it's time to go on home
The hunt is over"

Now he lived for the seasons, and I lived for the reasons
He would take me back up to those hills again
Just to be up there together, thought these times would last forever
But today the good Lord said to him…
"It's time to go, the hunt is over
Throw that old Winchester gun across your shoulder
I know it's been good, son, to be here in these woods
But it's time to come on home
The hunt is over" [27]

Notes

1. John Weiss, *The Whitetail Hunter's Almanac* (New York: Skyhorse, 2017), 19,25.
2. Steve Chapman, "Outdoor Poetry," © 2019 by Times and Seasons music.
3. Joe Riekers, "Nineteen of the Best (or Maybe the Worst) Deer Hunting Jokes," *Wide Open Spaces*, September 6, 2019, http://www.wideopenspaces.com/19-deer-hunting-jokes.
4. Steve Chapman, "First Winds of Autumn," © 1992 by Times and Seasons Music.
5. Steve Chapman, *A Look at Life from a Deer Stand Devotional* (Eugene, OR: Harvest House, 2009), 41.
6. Adapted from Steve Chapman, *Another Look at Life from a Deer Stand* (Eugene, OR: Harvest House, 2007), 157.
7. Steve Chapman, "Just Add Water," © 2010 by Times and Seasons Music.
8. Steve Chapman, "God's Gonna Keep You in His Sights," © 2016 by Times and Seasons Music.
9. Don Hicks, "Master of the Morning," © 2012 by Don Hicks, from Steve Chapman and Don Hicks, *Tell Me a Huntin' Story* (Eugene, OR: Harvest House, 2017), 57-58.
10. Joe Goodman and Steve Chapman, "Old GMC," © 2019 by Times and Seasons Music.
11. Steve Chapman, as quoted in Jay Houston and Roger Medley, *A Hunter's Field Notes* (Eugene, OR: Harvest House, 2012), 19.
12. Steve Chapman, "Moments of Heaven," © 2016 by Times and Seasons Music.
13. Steve Chapman, "That's What I Get," © 2020 by Times and Seasons Music.
14. W.L. Walker, "Longsuffering," ed. James Orr, *International Standard Bible Encyclopedia Online*, accessed July 27, 2020, http://www.internationalstandardbible.com/L/longsuffering.html.
15. Steve Chapman, "Be Ready," © 2002 by Times and Seasons Music.
16. Carter Bentley and Steve Chapman, "Nearly Sixty-Nine," © 2019 by Times and Seasons Music.
17. Steve Chapman, "Something My Dad Would Do," © 2019 by Times and Seasons Music.
18. Steve Chapman, *365 Things Every Hunter Should Know* (Eugene, OR: Harvest House, 2008), 104, 125.
19. Steve Chapman, "Baby, It's Turkey Time," © 2020 by Times and Seasons Music.
20. NIV.
21. Jaymi Heimbuch, "Beavers: Eight Things to Know About Nature's Most Impressive Landscape Engineers," Treehugger, updated June 5, 2017, http://www.treehugger.com/beavers-things-know -about-natures-landscape-engineers-4863345.
22. D. Jake Roberts, "Jake Roberts: Leave It to Beaver," *Scottsbluff Star-Herald*, January 11, 2020, http://starherald.com/opinion/columnists/jake-roberts-leave-it-to-beaver/article_13b72cb5 -b8e9-5fc9-a69c-b82bf1d9abad.html.
23. Riekers, "Deer Hunting Jokes."
24. Riekers, "Deer Hunting Jokes."
25. Steve Chapman, "We Have a City," © 2020 by Times and Seasons Music.
26. Steve Chapman, "When I Walk These Fields," © 2000 by Times and Seasons Music.
27. Steve Chapman, "The Hunt Is Over," © 2000 by Times and Seasons Music.

About the Author

Steve Chapman and his wife, Annie, are award-winning musicians who take their message of Christ-centered family to fans all over North America. Steve's enthusiasm for Jesus, family, hunting, and humor shine in his books, including *A Look at Life from a Deer Stand* (nearly 300,000 copies sold), *The Hunter's Cookbook* (with Annie Chapman), and *Great Hunting Stories*.

More Books from Steve Chapman

365 Things Every Hunter Should Know

52 Prayers for My Grandchild

Another Look at Life from a Deer Stand

Dad's Guide to Praying for His Kids, A

Down Home Wit and Wisdom

Great Hunting Stories

Hunt for Faith, The

Hunter's Cookbook, The

Hunter's Devotional, The

I Love You and I Like You

Look at Life from a Deer Stand Devotional

Look at Life from a Deer Stand Gift Edition, A

Look at Life from a Deer Stand, A

Look at Life from the Riverbank, A

My Dream Hunt in Alaska

One-Minute Prayers® for Hunters

Stories from the Deer Stand

Tales Hunters Tell, The

Tell Me a Huntin' Story

The Big Book of Hunting Stories, The

Wasn't It Smart of God to...

With Dad on a Deer Stand

To learn more about Harvest House books and
to read sample chapters, visit our website:

www.harvesthousepublishers.com

HARVEST HOUSE PUBLISHERS
EUGENE, OREGON